FLOWER CRAFT

To Mam.

From Catherine And Alexander.

For Mother's Day. 1978.

Marshall Cavendish London & New York

Picture Credits
A-Z Collection 11.
Theo Bergstrom 28.
Steve Bicknell 8,9,12,42,43,50,51,62,86.
Michael Boys 16.
Michael Boys/designed by
    John Stefanidis 11(r).
Camera Press 66.
Alan Duns 80,81.
Geoffrey Frosh·75,77(t).
Melvin Grey 37,38/9,82.
Graham Henderson 79.
David Hicks Ltd 17.
Chris Hollands 49(br),70/1.
Paul Kemp 4,56,77(b).
Chris Lewis 20/1,45,67.
Lutterworth Press 59.
Maison de Marie Claire/Godeaut 40.
Bill McLaughlin 34,54,63,69.
Dick Miller 25,26,48,49(bl),72/3,85.
Brian Morris 18(br),52.
Keith Morris 2,32,52.
Peter Pugh Cook 74(t).
Sale/Stone/Senior 7,11(cl & bl),13,14.
Kim Sayer 60.
Jessica Strang 23(bl).
Sungravure 64.
John Swannell 31.
Transworld 22.
Jerry Tubby 55,61.
Liz Whiting 53,58.
Michael Wickham 18,19,23(br),46.
ZEFA 57.

Edited by Yvonne Deutch

Published by Marshall Cavendish Books Limited,
58 Old Compton Street,
London W1V 5PA

© Marshall Cavendish Limited, 1970, 1971, 1972
1973, 1974, 1975, 1976, 1977

This material first appeared in other
Marshall Cavendish publications

First printing 1977

ISBN 0 85685 258 9

Printed in Great Britain by
Severn Valley Press Limited

Introduction

We all love flowers. They bring a sense of grace and beauty into our lives, and are a source of spontaneous joy and pleasure. Yet most of us recognize only one way of using them creatively – the art of flower arranging. In fact there is an extensive history of flower craft throughout the centuries. Country housewives of bygone days were well versed in all sorts of ingenious ways of using the flowers of the cottage garden and the hedgerow, and as well as displaying them decoratively, they found many ways of putting them to more prosaic use – as medicines, as foods, as beauty aids and as refreshing drinks.

Flowercraft is a treasury of this intriguing lore. Not only will you discover some beautiful examples of flower arrangements for both town and country settings, but also how to create enchantingly pretty posies and bouquets for weddings. You can learn the traditional ways of distilling your own perfumes and floral essences, as well as how to prepare soothing creams and potions from natural ingredients to keep your skin petal soft. If you enjoy cooking, you might like to try some of the unusual flower recipes included, such as rose petal ice cream and crystallized flowers. You can dry, preserve and press flowers, use them as pot pourri and as scented pillows and sachets, and even make your own fantasy flowers from fabric, paper, feathers and sea shells.

Full instructions are provided, with helpful diagrams and gorgeous illustrations which make *Flowercraft* a pleasure to read and use. Once you've tried some of the projects, you'll think about flowers in an entirely new way, as part of your own creativity which is as varied and lively as the blossoms themselves.

Contents

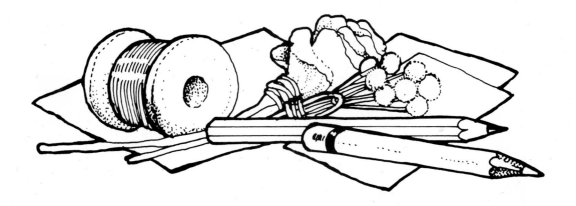

Flower arranging~
traditional
and modern themes

"Chevalier: I have always been fond of Flowers, but my Idea of their Merit was too mean and imperfect; I considered them as little productions that were accidentally scattered over the Earth. But I am now sensible they make their Appearance to please me, and I regard them with Admiration and Gratitude . . ."

Anon. *Nature Display'd*
Translated by Samuel Humphreys, 1766

Getting to know flowers

Anyone who is fascinated by colour and finds enjoyment in mixing different hues and blending new shades with existing ones – anyone in fact, who loves decoration and design – will find infinite pleasure in arranging flowers. It is one of the most decorative of the decorative arts.

You cannot keep rearranging a room all the time but you can make significant changes in it simply by rearranging the flowers. How you arrange them, the colours you choose, their size, the containers you put them in, all result in subtle or dramatic variations in mood and appearance. But just as your surroundings reflect your needs and individual style, so flowers should reflect the room's and this is the most important thing to bear in mind when arranging any flowers – that they must eventually become part of a room. They cannot exist simply as 'an arrangement' in splendid isolation.

Flowers and background

Styles of flower arrangement change with styles of home decoration and today the keynote is informality. Rigid, symmetrical lines have been replaced by more gentle contours and damask

has given way to printed cottons. Where simplicity and ease prevail these should be reflected in the flowers in a room. But there's more to apparent simplicity than meets the eye – the main thing being a good sense of proportion and harmony.

You are limited by four main considerations: the flowers available, the colours and spaces in your home, the containers you have and the reservoir of your own ideas. It also helps to learn to care for flowers properly, as arrangements can last twice as long with proper attention from the start.

Selecting flowers

The flowers you use depend largely on where you live, whether in town or in the country, and what time of year it is. But before you buy or pick flowers, even when they are in abundance, it makes sense to think about where you are going to put them, since both the colour and the size of the arrangement will be affected. A large, massed arrangement, for instance, requires an area such as a chest or table without a lamp on it, and colours must work together and also contribute to the room. In winter, when flowers are scarce and expensive, it is a good rule to stick to small arrangements of a few flowers of one kind such as carnations. Even one flower in the right container can make a successful arrangement, adding just the degree of colour needed for a finishing touch.

Expensive winter flowers can also be filled out with greenery, but really large spaces are probably best filled at this time of year with dried arrangements which can look superb.

Preparing flowers

Buy florist's flowers still in the bud if you can and avoid any with centres that look over-mature (blowsy, with

Stems become part of the arrangement when a glass container is used.

loose pollen, too dark in colour) or have drooping edges and leaves. As soon as you get them home, trim a thumbnail's length off the stems by making a slanting cut and plunge the stems into tepid water to soak.

Pick garden flowers before they are fully open and never during the full heat of a summer day. Never twist or pull the stem off but cut with special flower scissors, making a slanting, rather than straight, cut. Lupins [lupine] are an exception, they should be cut straight across. If you are picking many flowers then put a bucket of water in a shady place and put them into it as you cut. Plants, quite naturally, are shocked by cutting and jostling but gentle treatment seems to mollify them.

Wild flowers are the most delicate of all to maintain but the effort is well worth it. Go collecting equipped with a roll of kitchen foil, paper towels and a bottle of water. Wrap the stems in dampened paper and then cover with kitchen foil. Keep flowers out of the sun as much as possible after picking. Alternatively, tie them up in large plastic bags. It cannot be emphasized too strongly that when you are gathering wild flowers, you must check to make sure that you are not encroaching on a species which is at risk. What is more, *never* dig up wild flowers with their roots.

Prolonging life

A little extra care is well worth it in the response which flowers make, keeping their heads erect and leaves crisp and often doubling their life.

Soaking flowers in water up to their necks for several hours or overnight is a good thing to do before starting to arrange them in a container. Leaves (except for velvety ones) can also be submerged. Soft rain-water from a rain barrel is ideal. All water should be at room temperature before you put flowers in it.

Always arrange flowers in tepid water – a small piece of charcoal in the container will keep the water pure. Most flowers, except those that exude a sticky substance, such as daffodils, will last longer if you add some sugar to the water – two teaspoons to 600ml (1pt) [2½ cups]. Daffodils and narcissi can last very well in little water, as long as they do not go dry, but hellebore need deep water, or to be floated in a bowl. Holly is best without any water at all. But apart from a few exceptions, plants are not particularly fussy about exactly how much water they are arranged in. The water in vases should be filled up

The stylosa iris, arranged by David Hicks, illustrates basic principles of arranging flowers in the modern home. It is simple, natural looking and blends easily with its surroundings.

every day with fresh water at room temperature. The stems of lilac, roses and chrysanthemums should all be hammered and split about 2.5cm (1in) up the stem to let the water in.

Types of stems

Stems which exude a white juice, such as poppies and dahlias, should be put in a small dish of boiling water for about ten seconds to disperse the juice. Protect the heads by covering them with a cloth. Poppies can be discouraged from fading by charring the ends of the stalks.

Tulips only drink through the green part of their stems so cut off any white part at the base. They also tend to droop when arranged, and wrapping stems in newspaper up to the heads (putting no more than six in each bunch) before soaking them helps stiffen them. It's said also that tulips straighten up when they see themselves reflected in a mirror.

Wallflowers will die quickly on long stems, so cut them quite short. Daffodils and narcissi exude a sticky substance. Hold the stems under running water to remove it. This juice is harmful to other flowers so try to segregate this group or, alternatively, soak them for at least six hours before combining them with other flowers. If you cut broom when it is in flower put the stems in very hot water before arranging it in a container.

Carnation stems should be broken between the joints, not at the joints. Delphiniums and lupins [lupine] last longer if their hollow stems are filled with water after they are cut. Plug the stems with cotton wool [cotton] and leave overnight in deep water.

Cut hydrangeas on the new wood. Before arranging them, place the stems in boiling water for a few seconds. Then soak the flower heads in tepid water. Hydrangeas absorb water through the flower heads, so it helps to spray them frequently after they have been arranged. Mimosa also lasts

9

longer if sprayed in this way. Iris stems contain a lot of water and it is evaporation that causes them to droop. When picked, wrap each head in soft paper and place the flowers in deep water. Leave in a cool place for a few hours. Polyanthus lasts better if the stems are cut short and the flowers grouped together in a posy.

Although it is correct to soak flowers with leaves submerged, always remove any leaves below the waterline before you put them in a container. Leaves take up space and water unnecessarily. They also tend to discolour the water and make it smell foul. Thin out excess foliage so that flower heads are not starved of water.

Basic equipment

Flower scissors (fig. 1a) are an invaluable tool as their serrated edges make it possible to cut flowers, tough wood stems and wire mesh used in containers. Wire mesh (fig. 1b) is obtained at most gardening and some hardware shops and should be plastic coated, if possible, since this does not rust. Wire with 5cm (2in) holes is the most useful, and crumpled balls of it are excellent for holding arrangements erect. A little practice is needed, however, to get the right amount of mesh for the size of the vase and the flowers which need support. More than one layer of wire is necessary in tall vases and you will need to align the holes so that the flowers will go all the way into the container.

Pin holders (fig. 1c) are small round beds of nails that can be bought in several sizes and provide useful anchors for many kinds of arrangements. Put them into the container before the water and stick each stem securely into the nails. Sometimes it is necessary to attach the pin holder to the container with a bit of plasticine to keep it from sliding about. Even the smartest pin holder is less attractive than stems so avoid using them in clear glass vases.

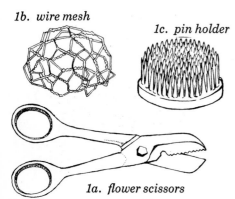

1b. wire mesh

1c. pin holder

1a. flower scissors

Containers

Choosing the right container is one of the most important elements in flower arrange for if it is wrong, then it will spoil everything else.

Containers should by no means be limited to those designed specially to hold flowers. They can be improvised from any number of household objects – imagine an earthenware jug full of wild flowers or a teapot full of sweet peas. Wicker baskets make very effective containers provided you use old cans as waterproof liners.

Glass containers are another intriguing possibility since the stems of flowers become part of the total line of the arrangement. A number of clear or tinted glass containers can be quickly obtained with a bottle-cutting device. By sawing off the top at the desired place you get containers of different heights and shapes.

Bowls of all sorts can be used to hold flowers when a pin holder or mesh is used for support, but shallow arrangements as a rule do not last as long as others of larger dimensions.

Correct proportions

Texture and colour are of immense importance in a container and so is size. As a general rule, in tall arrangements (but not large round ones) flowers should not protrude more than

50 per cent above the top of the container. Tall flowers look ridiculous in a short, stocky vase but the reverse is not true. It is perfectly permissible to have only the heads of flowers protruding beyond the lip of a tall vase. You will find you have many more creative possibilities working with flowers if you keep a selection of containers in the sizes, colours and textures which lend themselves to the mood of your home. Store them on a shelf or in a cupboard where you can tell at a glance what might and might not do. A list of improvised containers – eg silver coffee pot, galvanized pail, china cream jug – tucked inside the cupboard door will serve as a useful reminder of possibilities. A large part of thinking up ideas is, after all, having a quick cross-reference of the alternatives at your disposal.

Colour

There is perhaps nothing in nature as ornamental as flowers and when you think of arranging them, try thinking about them in their natural state first,

Below and opposite page: Choose your containers imaginatively so that they enhance flowers. Vases are available in all shapes and sizes, and can also be improvised from common household items. The kitchen will provide lots of ideas, so that you will never lack variety. Whatever container you choose, try to keep a pleasant proportion.

right

right

wrong

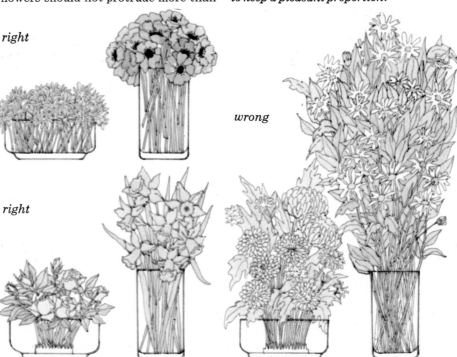

not in an orderly planted garden but in a field. Cast your mind back to fields of flowers or herbaceous borders you have seen and this will give you some idea of the tremendous scope you have in mixing and combining different colours and flowers in your home.

When buying flowers it is a good idea to keep these thoughts in mind and never buy the same number of each kind of flower, rather choose a dozen of one kind and perhaps half a dozen of another. If they can be bought singly get odd numbers. This will give you a more 'natural' look.

Making arrangements

By no means confine your efforts to putting flowers in a container one at a time although this may be necessary in those requiring a pin holder or wire mesh. Trim the lengths fairly evenly and try sticking a bunch into a vase all at once – giving a gentle shake – to get a natural look. If you are using greenery, stick it in amongst the flowers instead of 'backing them up' with it.

Remember that flowers are fragile and need gentle handling. Camellias and gardenias for example bruise easily and should be touched as little as possible.

Most flowers do best if any dead heads are removed – even freesias last longer this way – and it encourages other buds to open themselves up.

Be spontaneous

Laying down too many rules about arranging flowers defeats the whole concept of informality and whether or not you are successful with flowers depends as much on spontaneity as on anything. So don't be afraid to experiment, but bear in mind at the same time the basic guidelines about using display space and determining the mood of a room. A bunch of daisies in the hands of six different people can clearly

express six different personalities, provided each person has a definite idea of what they want the flowers to 'say'. This is far more important than any involved techniques. It is always worth reading books on flower arrangement, visiting flower shows and joining flower clubs, but in the end your own personal taste ought to be your best source of inspiration.

Below: Position your arrangements so that they are not overpowering.

Bottom: A gaily coloured summer posy arrangement makes a happy and light-hearted mood, created by deliberate use of asymmetry.

right

wrong

The formal tradition

Formal flower arrangements are by definition those that have some pre-determined shape or form to them. Unlike more simply arranged informal flowers they do not rely altogether on the natural beauty of colour and texture to make them aesthetically pleasing. They need careful planning to make them successful and the arranger's art shows both in the over-all shape and the positioning of each blossom and piece of foliage. Success depends upon composition and form and the flowers are the raw materials.

Over the years established guidelines have come to be accepted for formal flower arrangements and their rather traditional feeling is best reflected against a similar background.

The more informal atmosphere of most modern homes, and the time and expense involved in making carefully composed arrangements, has meant that formal flowers are now mainly 'special occasion' flowers for decoration at special events such as receptions, club dinners, official gatherings or church services.

Backgrounds

With all forms of flower arranging you must take the background into account because this will determine where the flowers are going to be – the colours, size and shape of arrangement. If you are arranging flowers for a church or a function in rooms with which you are already familiar, it will be a lot easier for you to select your flowers and plan the size and numbers of arrangements.

If the function is to be in a hotel, or other less familiar accommodation, visit the rooms, make notes on the colours of the walls and curtains and find out about the position of tables and any other furnishings that will affect your choice of flowers.

Always make a point of discussing with caterers the details of the china, table linen, and positioning of tables. White china on a white tablecloth may need vivid floral colours while a pastel cloth will probably look better with softer tones. You must also decide beforehand how many arrangements to make and how big each of them should be.

Dinner settings

Flowers for seated dinners should be low enough to allow guests to see each other over them. People sometimes use épergnes, or pedestal-mounted bowls to decorate dinner tables with splendid,

Escallonia, roses and single pinks can look very 'grand' arranged in a slightly formal manner.

cascading arrangements, but these also block the view of dinner guests opposite and this is a mistake no matter how beautiful the flowers.

For such occasions the best arrangements are low, rounded or elongated shapes and these can be made in shallow containers on a base of wire mesh or floral foam.

The number of table arrangements depends on the length of the table and whether candles are used. As a rule, a single centre arrangement with flanking candles is sufficient for up to 20 guests; longer tables may have two other smaller arrangements echoing the centre one. With U-shaped tables the same theme can be extended to the flanking tables.

Small groups

Some dinners are arranged with lots of small round tables and in this case identical centrepieces should be used. A tiny bouquet or a slender vase with a single rose or gladiolus is appropriate, although not really formal.

Flowers for receptions

Reception flowers probably give the greatest scope for floral opulence, but here again, background is important. If there is a mantelpiece you can use it as a natural focal point and place a small arrangement at either end. Chests, pedestals and large side tables are other obvious places and these can take the largest, grandest arrangements. These often present the biggest challenge to the arranger but can also be the most fun to do.

A large entrance hall is usually reserved for the most magnificent arrangement of all and this often takes the form of a large urn filled with a variety of flowers of many colours.

Flowers for church

Church flowers can be among the most satisfying of formal arrangements to do because of the enormous amount of space and light which create different effects. When arranging church flowers you must bear in mind the size, style and period of the church itself. Informal bouquets of wild flowers will look delightful in the small chapel of an ancient or rustic country church but would be totally out of place in a more imposing building. Most church flowers need clear form and shape.

Flowers, particularly those arranged at the chancel steps, must be large and high enough to be visible from the back of the church. It is also better in many cases to have flowers in all shades of one colour rather than in contrasting colours so the shape of the arrangement is sufficiently dominant.

Altar flowers present a difficulty because they often have to compete both with altar hangings and stained glass windows. But on the whole, the natural stone or whitewashed walls of many churches make them fine environments for appreciating the beauty of flowers.

Lime with its leaves stripped off, and Hosta Glauca leaves for bold contrast give an unusual touch to this fresh-coloured bowl. The arrangement is based on the classic triangular shape.

Design ideas

Many ideas are generated by our being responsive to our surroundings, and ideas about flower arrangements are no exception, so make a point of noticing the flowers you see around you. For example, do you find the arrangements you see satisfying, and if not, why not? Try to define what displeases or pleases you. Is it the positioning, shape, colours? By making these observations you become more aware of your own personal taste. Noting the colours in household furnishings or clothes can generate ideas about combining colours and tones in floral arrangements, but one of the best ways of getting ideas about creating elegant or luxuriant formal arrangements is to go to the library and look at illustrations of flower paintings, particularly seventeenth and eighteenth-century Dutch and French. Once you have begun to appreciate the vivid shape and colour through the artist's eye you will be able to look at your own arrangements and then expand your own visual ideas.

Formal arrangements

The outline or shape of formal arrangements is all-important and tra-ditionally the forms used are the circle and the triangle. Figs. 1–5 show variations of these two geometric shapes. Notice that the angles of the triangles differ, making broader or taller arrangements, and the crescent, as a part of the circle, is also used. The three basic steps to follow when attempting any arrangement are really extremely simple to understand.

The outline must be established first by putting in the tall outline material such as delphiniums, gladioli, forsythia, yew, lime (with the leaves stripped off), and grasses. Start by placing three pieces to fix the main outline points and then add a few more, if you wish, to complete the shape. In formal arrangements all the stems must appear to come from a single point so that the flowers seem to flow outward and upward from a single stem. Containers can form part of the whole or act as a kind of pedestal supporting the arrangement.

The centre of interest

Focal interest is created by the large blooms such as peonies, rhododendrons, magnolias, roses or tight clusters of berries are ideal, but avoid giving the effect of one central blob of colour. Choose flowers which will enhance but not totally dominate the arrangement. Large areas of dark colour tend to look heavy and should be kept in the centre.

Filling material, for example Sweet Williams, marguerites or sweet peas–is used to connect the heavier central flowers with the lighter outline. Do not be tempted, however, to fill in every single gap you can find. The effect of a flower arrangement can be ruined if it is too tightly packed. Most formal arrangements are designed to be viewed from only one angle and by pointing several stems slightly backwards, away from the front, a sense of fullness is created with few flowers.

Choosing flowers

Flowers in all stages, from buds to blossoms, can be used since lighter material must be mixed with the heavy to give grace and elegance. Think about the texture of the flowers and leaves. Leaf texture always affects the weight and balance of an arrangement. A shiny leaf could be used with great effect as a highlight. Do not use strongly textured leaves as outline material, unless they are very pale in colour and therefore visually light, or your arrangement will look top heavy. If possible always have odd numbers of different flowers. Large blooms can usually be bought singly, but many flowers are sold in bunches of even numbers. These can be split up, however, if more than one arrangement is involved.

Figs. 1-5. Formal arrangements usually have geometric shapes. Note the variations of the circle and the triangle shown here.

Flowers for city people

The average apartment or recently-built house in a town tends to have small rooms and compact furniture – not much scope for outsize arrangements, nor a casual brimming-over look. Probably florists' flowers – few because of their cost – will be the material used. As for foliage, it is usually possible to find some on a country walk or in a friend's garden. Even with such limitations, however, a distinctive style can be created, appropriate to the setting.

Making the most of space

To make the most of limited space, use snowdrops in miniature arrangements, or lily-of-the-valley, freesias, ranunclus, pinks and crocuses and put these on a desk top, dressing table or hall windowsill. Small urns are particularly suited to miniature arrangements, giving them extra importance.

Neat foliage in miniature arrangements can be provided by sprigs of broccoli or parsley, or leaves from a peperomia plant. With delicately coloured flowers like pinks, skeleton magnolia leaves (from a florist or garden centre) could be used, sprayed white or silver. On a small dining table, such flowers could be wired into a long garland and laid (with candles) along the centre (or in a circle) just before the meal starts, having been kept in water meanwhile. Some flowers, because they remain tidy and do not sprawl, are well suited to a modern flat [apartment]. Hyacinths for example,

with some large ivy leaves for contrast; massed anemones or marigolds cut short; lilies with laurel leaves and Solomon's Seal; carnations, not with the over-used asparagus fern but among holly leaves. A solitary branch or two of blossom, eucalyptus, pussy willow or chestnut buds may be all that is needed to make a corner of a room interesting, relying on linear composition to provide all the decoration that is needed. In autumn, Symphoricarpus (Snowberries) (white) and Pyracantha or Cotoneaster berries (red) add fresh interest; or use bare branches painted white to enhance their shape.

Combining flowers

Florists' flowers can be made more of, not only with cultivated foliage but with wild kinds brought home after a drive in the country. Add black hypericum berries to a bowl of red tulips, for instance, or even use a froth of Chaerophyllum Sylvestre (cow parsley) heads in a shallow dish on a coffee table, or an all-foliage group.

Stylized arrangements

A very stylized effect can be created by buying a large ball or cone of flower arranging foam or making one of chicken wire (foam-filled) and entirely covering the surface with flower heads (marguerites, polyanthus or anemones are a good choice). Such a ball of flowers can be hung up on a ribbon, or be placed on top of a short white rod held rigid in a flowerpot of compost or sand. Cones of yellow roses, grapes and ivy set on a pair of urns would be a handsome addition to a formal mantelpiece, and so would redcurrants among white nicotiana (tobacco plant).

Opposite: For a formal room with large pieces of furniture, a group of elegant lilies is very effective. This is a good example of florist's flowers combined with country foliage.

Left: The lily again, but this time used in an entirely different mood. David Hicks composed this casual bunch of flowers for his city flat, mingling together a well-chosen group of florist's flowers in a much more relaxed style. As usual, his arrangement is perfectly in harmony.

1

2

3

4

5

Countryside chic

If you live in town, you usually have to make do with bunches of one or two sorts of flowers and work with a limited palette of colour, texture and shape. But if you're fortunate enough to have a country garden, then you can build up a much richer mixture of blooms

The modern trend towards a more informal approach to flower arranging is seen in these photographs. A simple jug of flowers—either of mixed colours (1 and 6), or tones of one colour, (4 and 5), looks lovely on a window-ledge or table. Make use of natural light—its radiance streaming through a glass container is part of the charm of this arrangement (2). Sunlight through a door throws giant poppy leaves into relief (3). And a mass of lady's mantle enhances the delicacy of pinks.

and buds, mixed with leafy herbs or flowering branches.

The country house way of arranging flowers is usually similar to the style for town house, with the same emphasis on carefully planned balance, the same types of vases and containers – altogether more studied than a cottage posy or the modern decorator's understated bunches.

Country cottage styles

Even in town some homes manage to achieve a nostalgically countrified look – with simple pine furniture, oak chests and homespun curtains. In surroundings like these, formal flower arrangements would strike the wrong note. Cottage garden flowers are a good

choice: marguerites, lupins [lupine], delphiniums, cornflowers, honeysuckle, anemones, daffodils, primroses, marigolds, pinks, stocks, nasturtiums and the like. Supplement these with wild flowers; and in autumn pick berries from the hedgerows: bryony, hawthorn, elder, rosehips and blackberries still greeny-red, to use with trails of ivy and old man's beard. In spring, arrange primroses or crocuses among moss and ferns for charming effect.

Containers

Containers should be in keeping – simple white pottery, an old blue and white patterned teapot, baskets (with a water pot or tin inside), a child's mug, even an old pair of scales. A shiney new galvanized bucket would have a certain splendour brimming with pink peonies and mauve lilac.

For the country cottage look, small arrangements look best as little rounded posies rather than in more contrived pyramids or asymmetrical shapes. For large jugs or pots the aim should still be soft and artless, with the stems cut roughly the same length.

6

7

The painter's touch

At different periods and in different countries, distinct styles of flower arrangement have emerged. The ancient Egyptians decorated rooms with cut flowers (mostly the lotus, a water lily) and the Romans used festoons of roses.

Ideas from the past

It can be fun to browse through art books of a particular period, or to do a little detective work in an art gallery, in order to spot, in paintings of interiors, just how the flowers used to be done – particularly if you have a room with furniture of a certain period.

Some really good films set in the past are executed with much care to get historical detail right: keep an eye open for the flower arrangements in them when you visit the cinema or watch television.

Flowers in art and decor

Flower varieties in Europe were few in medieval times; even such familiar ones as daffodils, tulips, lilacs and pinks had yet to be introduced. But a solitary white lily in a pewter jug (from a fifteenth-century painting now in New York) and branches of fir with colourful lilies and roses (painted by Raphael on a ceiling in Rome) are appealing ideas.

Voluptuous groups of rambler roses in soft colours, in the style of Boucher (who decorated La Pompadour's boudoir) would strike the right note among rococo French furniture or Sèvres porcelain of the eighteenth century. Sprays or cherry blossom might be placed on a piece of chinoiserie furniture, or beneath an old Japanese print hanging on the wall. Urns of fruit and laurel leaves would enhance French Empire furniture.

Chrysanthemums would look well in a room in which a fabric with a William Morris chrysanthemum pattern had been used for the curtains. Stylized Victorian posies might suit a mahogany table laid with Victorian cutlery. Huge sunflowers could decorate a room in which there was a print of Van Gogh's Sunflower picture, Josiah Wedgwood (who even wrote a pamphlet on how to arrange flowers) designed urn-shaped vases specially for them. Filled with graceful and loosely composed arrangements, these complement the Chippendale or Sheraton furniture of Wedgwood's own time.

For a twenties look, use a simple and very plain curve of flowers in a geometric container of rough pottery or thick glass.

Dutch painter look

Perhaps most striking of all period styles was the late seventeenth-century Dutch style. There was then a fashion amongst Dutch painters like Van Huysum for huge pictures of mixed flowers, in a free and spontaneous conglomeration which has a very exuberant look. The whole effect is of a great mass, rich in colour and variety – a deep and rather open arrangement always slightly disarranged. Outsize roses, peonies and tulips feature prominently. Strangely, the Dutch who liked these flower arrangement pictures did not then go in for real flower arrangements in their homes.

Achieving this look of abundance depends upon several necessities: plenty of space for its display, a big container, and huge quantities of flowers. If you do not have a bottomless pocket, a brimming garden (supplemented by hedgerow flowers and plants) is essential as a source of supply.

A Tudor touch

Easier (and cheaper) to copy is the Tudor custom of a small nosegay of herbs and scented flowers in every bedroom. This was believed to be healthy and is certainly a pleasure at bedtime – especially in a guest's room.

Like a seventeenth century still-life, the colours glow richly.

Unusual table settings

Side-table setting

Below is a pretty setting which was inspired by an attractive print of a flower arrangement. The print may have been discovered after many pleasurable hours spent browsing around antique shops, or it may have been a forgotten heirloom in the attic. By studying the style of the print the designer has interpreted it in a three-dimensional table display. In this case a cup and saucer similar in shape were found. Then appropriate flowers were arranged to repeat the picture's shape and form – the artist's still life is thus

given new dimensions.
By carefully adding more flowers and other decorative items an eye-catching side-table setting has been created.

Tussie Mussies

These little nosegays can be made of either fresh or dried flowers and herbs, but should be as sweet smelling as possible. They were carried up until the eighteenth century both for their perfume to ward off the evil smells which abounded – and also because they were thought to be a protection against

infection. And in England judges still carry a traditional Tussie Mussie made up of herbs.
There are endless variations of herbs or flowers which can be used to make up a Tussie Mussie. Usually, however, you start with a small flower like a rosebud, round it you put feathery silvery leaves like Artemisia or Centaurea Maritima and tie the bunch with wool or strong cotton thread. Around this put a circle of marjoram or thyme, then a round of mint, lavender or rosemary, then perhaps lemon balm and a row of astrantia flowers. Finish off with a circle of geranium or sage leaves and tie the whole tightly. It is worth remembering that if they are made with freshly-picked herbs, Tussie Mussies will dry well and keep their scent, so they make delightful presents. While for an unusual touch to a dinner party you could put a tiny Tussie Mussie by each place setting.

Unusual arrangements, either for dining or side tables are a pleasure to invent. These three examples are just a sample of the kinds of effects that can be achieved with a little ingenuity. Opposite: Cabbage, radishes and artichoke heads act as a centre-piece, and the small jugs of flowers reflect the vegetable colours.

Left: A 'three-dimensional' effect using pinks.

Below: Traditional Tussie Mussies make sweet place settings.

The Oriental tradition

The contemplation of beauty has long been an essential element in the culture of Japan, and the art of Ikebana arises out of it. The very simplicity of Ikebana arrangements is partly to allow the contemplation of each flower, branch and leaf, and a mass of flowers and foliage would be spiritually indigestible to the Japanese.

Ikebana means, quite literally, 'living flowers' but over the centuries it has come to refer to a way of arranging them using an exciting dimension altogether missing in Western-style flower arrangements. In Ikebana it is not just visual beauty that is important but also beauty of expression. Flowers, grasses, reeds, and shrubs all have their own symbolic meanings and by using this 'language of plants' within the basic laws of Ikebana it is possible to express mood and personal philosophy in flower arrangements just as in poetry and literature. Ikebana has become increasingly popular in the West and goes particularly well with modern furniture.

History of Ikebana

The art of flower arranging in Japan goes back to the sixth century when the Buddhist religion was introduced from China and with it the ritual of offering flowers to the Buddha, usually in great bronze vessels.

By the tenth century a school had been founded to teach these ritual arrangements, based on keeping the lines and shapes of nature and observing the intrinsic harmony of the universe. The early arrangements, called *Rikka*, were huge, up to 4.5m (15ft) tall, and very formal in appearance; but although they became much altered with time, the basic premises regarding the harmony and balance of nature remained in Ikebana as in Buddhism.

The practice of offering flowers to the Buddha soon spread from the temple to the homes of nobles and dignitaries and, of necessity, the style of arrangements became simplified and smaller in size so as to occupy the Tokonoma, the alcove sacred to Buddha in the Japanese household. This was a kind of domestic shrine.

Moribana

Eventually other adaptations were also made but none were more significant than those in the nineteenth century.

For the first time flower arranging became a female occupation as well as a male one and it was soon an expected accomplishment in any young woman. At this time also, a new style developed, called Maribana, which used shallow containers, thereby giving more freedom in arrangements. For the first time Ikebana moved out of the traditional alcove or Tokonoma and into the three-dimensional environment of the home, thus further broadening the scope for creating designs. Before this, arrangements had been visible from only one angle, now they could be contemplated from all around and from above. Moribana is still one of the most popular styles of Ikebana.

Symbolism

In order to 'speak' with flowers it is necessary to know what the symbols mean and although it would take some time to learn the complete Japanese flower vocabulary we can automatically understand a great many.

Poets have always drawn metaphors from nature, and in much the same way Ikebana uses the actual material of nature to make a poetic statement. As Shakespeare, for example, describes oncoming age or death as a time 'When yellow leaves, or none, or few, do hang Upon those boughs', so the Japanese flower arranger might express the same sentiment by actually putting branches on which only a few leaves remain into a container.

The three basic symbols

There are, in Ikebana, three basic symbols on which all arrangements are built and every 'story' told. Ikebana arrangements are made up of three main stems which respectively symbolize Heaven, Man and Earth. Other stems have a supporting role only (and there are special instances where

'Man' is removed and only two stems make up an arrangement).

Against this universal stage, expressions of all moods and outlooks are possible by the addition of not just flowers but many other natural materials – branches, grasses, rocks, driftwood, shells. All have their special meanings and many are universally familiar: the delicate peach blossom represents womanly beauty and modesty, the upright iris stands for bravery, and the lotus – one of the earliest flowers associated with Buddha – denotes nobility and sincerity. On the whole, grasses tend to be masculine, blossoms feminine.

Seasonal symbols

Just as important are the seasonal symbols. Autumnal leaves and torn leaves convey decline, sadness. Tight buds, half-opened ones and full-blown flowers show the time of future, present and past. The correct seasonal content of an arrangement is also important in Japan and no flower or plant is put into an arrangement that is not naturally in season. This is less important in Western countries, however, since the differences between indoors and out is more pronounced.

Making arrangements

Although several styles of arrangements are being taught today in some 2000 Ikebana schools in Japan alone, the best-known and most widely used styles are the Moribana, which uses a shallow container, and the Nageire, dating from an earlier time, which uses a tall container. The same basic principles apply to both.

In both Maribana and Nageire the three symbolic stems, Heaven, Man and Earth can be arranged in one of two styles – upright or slanting – to make natural-looking designs. In the upright, Heaven is always the highest stem, then Man, then Earth. But in the slanting style, man is exalted and placed at a higher angle than Heaven. Other materials keep the same relationship as found in nature: a tree branch is never placed lower than a flower and grasses never higher than a tree. The length of each stem is governed by certain laws as is the angle the stems are arranged at.

Types of arrangements

In keeping with the requirement for

simplicity, no more than three different types of materials are used in any one arrangement and uneven numbers of flowers are considered more aesthetic as well as being lucky. The latter is often disregarded in Western Ikebana since flowers are often sold in even numbers and even the most sincere Ikebana master, being Buddhist and believing all plant life to be sacred, would not condone the waste of a flower which has already been cut.

Basic equipment

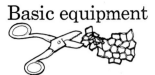

The success of an arrangement depends very much on the proper container and the securing of the plants. Containers are an integral part of the arrangement and should blend as much as possible with it. Earthy tones of green, grey or beige are safe to start with. Texture is also important and china, pottery, metalware or wood can all be used, depending on the statement being made.

For Moribana the container must be shallow and flat, but deep enough to hold two or three inches of water.

Three basic stems representing Man, Heaven and Earth are the central concepts of the Japanese tradition of flower arranging.

Nageire is, of course, much taller, but in both types the height of the arrangement will be determined by the diameter of the lip of the container.

The Japanese normally use a small wooden stand, *dai*, to support the container on a table but this is often dispensed with in the West.

Using pinholders

A pinholder or Kenzan (fig. 1a) is needed, especially in shallow Moribana arrangements. Heavy branches can be secured by diagonal cuts to fit into the kenzan along with flowers and other materials (fig. 1b). If a stem is particularly weighty then one kenzan can be placed upside down on the side of the other to balance it (fig. 1c).

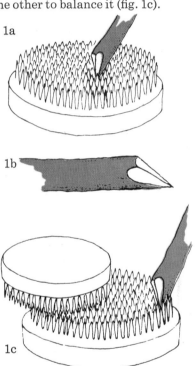

1a

1b

1c

Positioning holders
Kenzans should never be glued to containers since minute adjustments are usually required up to the last minute. Moreover, kenzans are never placed in the centre of a Moribana container as this would appear too carefully planned and 'unnatural'. In tall arrangements wire mesh is sometimes used or a counterbalance system (fig. 2) using a separate stick as an anchor. Florists' foam is also useful for embedding tall plants in vases.

In Ikebana, proper flower scissors with

Above: Using a kenzan or pin holder.

Right: Nageire arrangements are usually in tall containers.

serrated edges are a great asset and a sharp knife is also helpful to cut through or whittle down thick wooden stems. You will also need a protractor for measuring angles.

Moribana

These arrangements are both attractive to look at and easy for beginners. They look best on a low table which is free from other distracting objects, and the background should be as simple as possible.

Suggested combinations
Beech branches and daffodils, tree ivy and tulips, pussy willow and jonquils. Select an appropriate container and a kenzan which will be heavy enough to secure your arrangement.

Cutting the stems
Measure the width of your container and the depth. In a standard arrangement 'Heaven' will be equivalent in stem-length to the width of the container plus the depth and up to half as much again (depending on personal choice).
'Man' is three-quarters of the length of 'Heaven' and 'Earth' is three-quarters as long as 'Man'.
Supporting stems or fillers are never as long as the main stem and should be different lengths from each other.

Creating angles
Remove any unwanted leaves and trim branches to suit the curve you want to make. Branches can often be bent to emphasize a curve by carefully bending and twisting at the same time. Angles are measured from upright zero as shown in fig. 3 and those used are the constant angles of 10°, 45° and 75°. The distance between the tips of the stems should be consistent with the degree of angle required (fig. 3c).

Using camouflage
In Moribana the kenzan must always be invisible at a distance of a metre (yard) from the arrangement. This must often be done by using camouflage such as leaves, moss, pebbles.
In slanting arrangements a windswept look is achieved. 'Man' stands above 'Heaven' and 'Earth', eg 'Man' is at an angle of 10° from vertical zero (fig. 3a), 'Heaven' is 45° and 'Earth' is 75°.
In upright arrangements 'Heaven' is at an angle of 10° and 'Man' is 45° (a reversal of the above). In both, 'Earth' is 75° from vertical zero (fig. 3b).
Placement of the stems in the rear, side or foreground of arrangements varies.

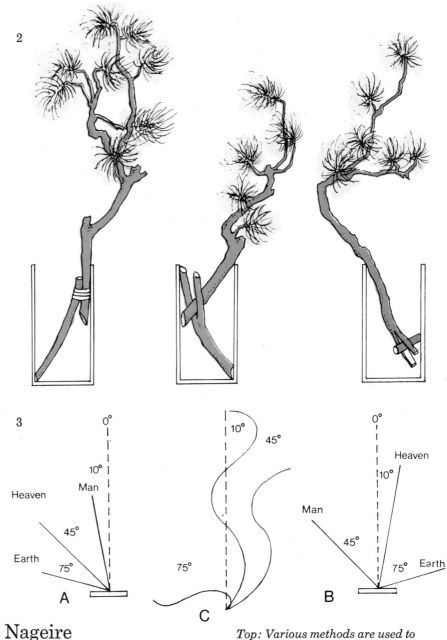

Top: Various methods are used to achieve the correct angle.

Above: In slanting arrangements (a) 'Man' is higher than 'Heaven' and 'Earth', while in upright kinds (b) 'Heaven' is higher than 'Man'. Each stem must measure exactly the angles indicated, and distance between the tops of each stem must be the degree of angle indicated (c.)

Nageire

Basically, Nageire is like Moribana but it is a bit more difficult to work arrangements in a tall container. The results, however, are worth it and are perhaps the best suited of all Ikebana styles to Western interiors.

Suggested combinations
Oak branches and roses or jonquils. Bare branches with chrysanthemums. Willow branches with tulips.
In Nageire, special balancing techniques must often be used to get an asymmetrical effect (fig. 2).
The length of the stems is determined, as in Moribana, by measuring the diameter of the top of the container and its depth and adding the two together. This gives the length of the

'Heaven' stem. For extra height it is possible to add up to half as much again but you must also allow for the amount of stem which will be submerged in the vase and the length of this will depend on your method of fixing it in the container.
In Nageire, larger flowers can be used than in the more delicate Moribana, because of the height of the container. In either, a splendid scope exists for poetic and decorative expression.

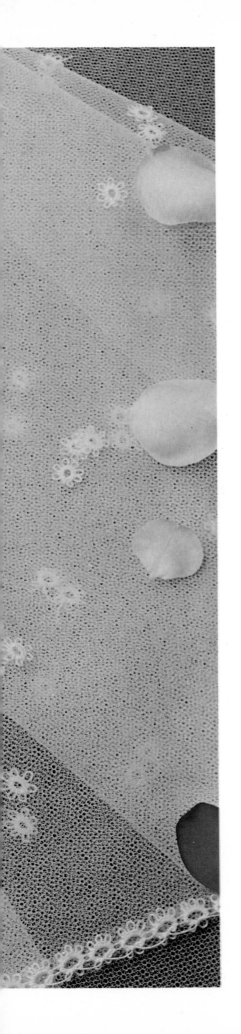

Wedding flowers

"*I sing of brooks, of blossoms, birds and bowers;*
Of April, May, of June and July-flowers.
I sing of May-poles, Hock-carts, wassails, wakes,
Of bridegrooms, brides, and of their bridal cakes."

Robert Herrick *Hesperides* 1591-1674

Flowers for weddings

Easily the best known use of festive flowers today is undoubtedly at weddings where bridesmaids' flowers, the bridal bouquet and often the floral head-dress form an integral part of the traditional ceremony.

A bouquet is really just a bunch of flowers tied together. It is the way in which it is arranged and presented that gives it a special quality.

Informal bouquet

An informal bouquet can consist of several flowers of the same kind – long-stemmed roses, for instance – tied together with a ribbon, or it can be a collection of small flowers joined into a posy for a child to carry. The word bouquet is derived from the French word 'bois', meaning a wood, and probably referred originally to bunches of wild flowers gathered there.

Formal bouquet

A formal bouquet, however, is a skillful preparation, using wire to give the maximum control in creating the effect. Formal bouquets can be different shapes and sizes and consist of both natural-stemmed flowers and flowers with false stems made from covered wire, or, in the case of very formal bouquets, all the flowers can be mounted on false, wired stems.

Choosing bridal flowers

The secret of a good bouquet lies in the choice of flowers and foliage used against the dress material, its lightness, the way it balances in the hand and also its movement. Flowers at all stages of growth should be used since buds and half-opened flowers make for lightness in appearance and also help to maintain a well-proportioned visual balance, which is very important.

Shapes and textures

A bouquet is better if it is made up of not too many different pieces; the shape and texture of the flowers are also important.

In wedding bouquets the basic shapes are the straight or curved hand shower, the crescent spray, loose posy and the Victorian posy, where all the flowers are in rings around a central rose bud.

Flowers for bouquets

White flowers which can be used include lily of the valley, hyacinth pips, white freesia, white anemones, bride gladioli, white or Christmas roses, nerine, white spray carnations (not the large-flowered single stems), eucharis lily, small arum, single spray chrysanthemums, white stock, gardenia, longiflorum lily, white delphinium, stephanotis, orange blossom, white orchids (odontoglossom vanda phalenopsis).

Coloured flowers

Coloured flowers are easier because they provide an even wider choice and many subtle colours can be blended. Particularly beautiful colours are found in hybrid nerine, orchids, and gerbera. The single spray chrysanthemums, spray carnations, baby gladioli and freesia are all suitable flowers for bouquets and posies.

Foliage

Foliage is an important part of many bouquets and such leaves as baby begonia rex, peperomia, geranium, eucalyptus, senecio, veronica, tradescantia and the many different forms of ivy are all useful for highlighting flowers and acting as contrast.

Care of flowers

All flowers and foliage to be used in a formal bouquet must be fully charged with water before wiring; once they are wired they have no chance of taking up more water and rely only on overhead spraying to keep them fresh. Therefore soak all flowers up to their necks for several hours before wiring them into their final shape.

No bouquet will last for very long, but the lifespan of flowers varies to some degree. For instance, lily of the valley looks sad fairly quickly, whereas orchids will hold up for two to three days with reasonable care.

It is sometimes possible to preserve a bouquet after the ceremony by placing it in an airtight bag containing silica-gel crystals, obtainable from pharmacies. See also chapter on preserving.

Wiring

It is wiring which distinguishes a formal bouquet, but flowers can be easily ruined by being badly wired. Special florist's wire comes in different gauges and, as a rule, the lightest wire which will hold a flower satisfactorily should be used. Over-wiring makes a bouquet look stiff and heavy; the wires should hold the flowers gracefully in position, not act as stakes.

Types of wire

Two types of wire are used in floral bouquets, stubb wires and silver reel wire. (Sizes in mm and B & S gauges.) Stubb wires act as stalks or false stems and resemble long, thin needles. They come in several lengths and thicknesses but are normally between 18cm (7in) and 36cm (14in) long.

Silver reel wire is a fine wire used for binding flowers together or preparing them for stubb wire. Silver wire comes in several gauges – the higher the gauge, the finer the wire.

All florist's wire can be purchased from floral supply houses but if you only want a small quantity try to persuade your local florist to sell you a supply.

How to wire

Basic ways to wire flowers and foliage are shown in figs. 1–12.

Normally flowers must be pierced through the head with silver reel wire, the wire end twisted together and then left hanging to form two 'legs' about 8cm (3in) long (fig. 1). It is these 'legs' that will be used later to attach the flower to the false stem (stubb wire). Figs. 2–7 show different ways to pierce the heads and petals of flowers and foliage or bind them together with reel wire.

Occasionally a heavy bud or flower is wired directly onto a stubb wire or false stem by the method shown in fig. 8, thus giving the flower support and doing away with step one.

Unless otherwise directed, always cut away all but about 2.5cm (1in) of the natural stem. The remaining stem is used for twisting silver wire around.

Using tape

Gutta percha is a special tape made from rubber and used to cover false stems. It comes in green, white and skin tone and can be bought, like florist's wire, from floral supply houses. Gutta percha does not need to be tied off since it sticks to itself. It is normally applied by spiral binding down the stem to cover it.

A pair of florist's scissors with serrated edges and a fine water spray are two other essentials in making formal bouquets.

Making a head-dress

You will need:
1 very narrow head band
4 sprays of artificial white orchids with two flowers on each spray (or similar flowers)

1 bunch small white artificial roses
1.85m (2yd) each of 0.6cm (¼in) apple green and white ribbon
A small quantity of white wool
0.90m (1yd) of 29cm (11½in) wide milliners net

A bridal head-dress of fresh flowers is enchantingly pretty and very easy to make.

If preferred fresh flowers may be substituted. Freesia, lily of the valley, maidenhair fern, white heather, orchids and miniature gladioli would all be suitable.

Arrange two sprays of orchids on each side of the head band, placing the flowers so that the general shape tapers towards the neck. Hold in position with small pieces of cellophane tape. Separate the white heather and roses and insert heather between the orchids, again holding in place with tape. Arrange roses along the head band. Starch the ribbon so that it is firm enough to stand on its own and arrange in loops between the orchids. Try on the head dress.

Wind the wool around the stalks and band, binding them together and covering the tape.

Cut the length of net in half. Fold down 12.5cm (5in) along one long edge on each piece. Gather the folded edge in the hand and wind a double length of thread tightly around the net approximately 2.5cm (1in) from the fold, leaving the ends of the thread long enough to tie the gathered net behind the flowers on either side of the head-dress.

A child's head-dress

You will need:
Silver reel wire in 0.28mm (gauge 29).
Baby ribbon, 1.5m (1½yd).
1 large head hydrangea (small flowered).
6 stems paper white narcissi.
2 large carnations.
Ivy foliage.
36cm (14in) covered milliner's wire, available from milliner's supply shop, or use two 36cm (14in) stubb wires.
Gutta percha tape and scissors.

Make the circle frame by bending the milliner's wire into a circle and overlapping the ends by 1.5cm (½in), or bind two stubb wires together with silver wire, wrap gutta percha around them and bend to form a circle.

Bind silver wire and then gutta percha around the overlap to hold ends together and form a complete circle to which flowers will be added one at a time in sequence.

To wire flowers.
Each flower must be wired with silver reel wires cut to lengths of about 15cm (6in). You can vary the amount and

Top: Bride's hand shower.

Right: Child's posy and head-dress.

1. Wire 'legs' for mounting flowers are made by piercing part of the flower or leaf, twisting the wire around the cut stem and leaving two 'legs' 8cm (3in) long.

2. Different flowers are pierced in different places; roses through lower bud.

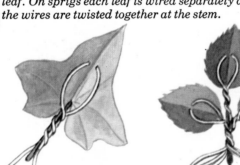

6. Lily of the valley, veronica and ivy trails are wired by twisting silver wire down the stem, taking care not to break them.

7. Single leaves are wired by piercing the back of the leaf. On sprigs each leaf is wired separately and then all the wires are twisted together at the stem.

types of flowers shown here or use different ones altogether, still following the diagrams showing different methods of wiring.

Paper white narcissi.
Cut flowers from the main stem and pierce each blossom, through its base with silver wire (fig. 5), twisting the ends together and leaving two 'legs' hanging down (fig. 1).

Hydrangea.
Pick two or three flowers from the large round head and bind them together to make a tiny bunch (fig. 4). Make several of these.

Carnation.
Flowers are normally used whole but carnations are an exception because sometimes they are too large for the arrangement. Peel back the base of a flower and pull out a few petals. Place 3 or 4 on top of each other and bind with silver wire (fig. 3).

Ivy.
Pierce and bind each leaf (fig. 7).
To mount flowers on frame, hold the frame between thumb and forefinger with the other side of the circle resting on your wrist.
Place on the flowers and foliage one at a time, binding the 'legs' as one wire around the frame (fig. 9). Flowers should overlap slightly to give a thick effect. Work round all but 1.5cm (½in) of the frame and tie your ribbons on to the remaining space.

3. Carnation petals can be wired together to make a miniature blossom.

4. Wire hydrangeas by twisting a few florets into one blossom.

8. Sometimes a heavy bud or large flower is mounted directly onto a false stem or stub wire as shown in the illustration.

9. The 'legs' of silver wire secure flowers to frame as shown.

5. Narcissus and stephanotis are wired through the base, sometimes two together.

10. Silver wire also binds 'legs' to stub wire which is covered with floral tape.

11. Heavy blossoms are mounted on one stub wire, then fixed to a longer one.

12. Parts of a spray are wired individually, then put together again.

Victorian Posy

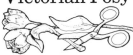

You will need:
Stubb wire, 0.56mm (gauge 23)×17.5cm (7in) long.
Silver reel wire, 0.31mm (gauge 28) and 0.28mm (gauge 29).
Posy frill or paper doily.
Gutta percha tape and scissors.
1.37m (1½yd) ribbon.
Flowers
1 large rosebud for centre.
7 rosebuds.
1 hydrangea.
2 carnations.
Buds of border carnations.
Victorian posies are made by arranging circles of different types of flowers, usually of a different colour, around one central flower (in this case a rose) and finishing off with a lacy frame.
For posy on page 32. The centre rose is wired by cutting off the stem to 1.5cm (½in) below the sepals (the bump above the stem) and piercing through the ovary (ie the seed box) (fig. 8). Use stubb wire for extra strength.
The first circle is of carnation buds wired with 0.31mm (gauge 28) silver wire. Pierce lower part of bud (fig. 2).
For the second circle: rosebuds are wired as above, but this time use 0.28mm (gauge 29) silver wire.
For the third circle: use hydrangea, wired with 0.28mm (gauge 29) silver wire by binding three or four flowers from a head (fig. 4).
For the fourth circle: peel three or four carnation petals from the head of a flower and place them on top of one another. Pierce and wire (fig. 3).

Binding the bouquet

To bind the bouquet together using 0.31mm (gauge 28) silver wire. Start with central rose and wrap wire around it a few times. Then begin to add other flowers in order of rows, working wire twice around each circle before adding the next one. The wire 'legs' of the flowers make a central 'stem'.
Bind in a circular motion keeping the silver reel wire in one place until all the flowers have been included, then take the silver wire in a spiral to the end of the 'stem'.
When the posy is completely bound, trim the central 'stem' to about 11.5cm (4½in), slip on the doily and cover the remaining 'stem' by wrapping gutta percha round it. Ribbons can now be tied on the 'stem' or 'handle' to complete the bouquet.

Opposite: An exquisite posy.

Fig. 13: Diagrams show how a wedding bouquet is built up from the bottom.

The posy on page 34 is made similarly, with circles of greenery and tiny flowers surrounding the centre bloom.

Hand shower

You will need:
Stubb wires, about a dozen 0.71mm (gauge 21)×36cm (14in) and about a dozen 0.57mm (gauge 24)×25cm (10in).
Silver reel wire in 0.31mm, 0.28mm, 0.20mm (gauges 28, 29, 32).
White gutta percha tape.
1.5m (1½yd) nylon taffeta ribbon 2.5cm (1in) wide.
Flowers
10 stems lily of the valley.
24 pips of stephanotis.
10 white roses with leaves.
5 trails of ivy.
1 pot veronica.

To wire flowers

For lily of the valley, the stem itself is wired as shown in fig. 6. Use 0.20mm (gauge 32) silver wire and start at the bottom of the stem, gently twisting wire upwards between the bells. Great care is needed to avoid pulling too tightly and cutting the stem.
Stephanotis is wired through the base

a   b

of the flower (fig. 5) using 0.28mm (gauge 29) silver wire.
Roses must have stems cut to varying lengths of between 5cm (2in) and 15cm (6in) and are then wired with 0.57mm (gauge 24) × 25cm (10in) stubb wires (fig. 8) to give the flowers enough support. Cut the stubb wires to the length of each natural stem.
Rose leaves should be wired in sprigs of three but each leaf in the sprig must be wired separately (fig. 7). Use 0.28mm (gauge 29) silver wire.
Ivy trails are wired like lily of the valley by twisting 0.20mm (gauge 32) silver wire around the natural stem (fig. 6).
Veronica is kept in natural sprays and wired with 0.31mm (gauge 28) silver wire wound around the stem like ivy trails (fig. 6).

Mounting the flowers.

Once you have prepared the pieces with silver wire they must be mounted on false stems of stubb wire and then each stem must be bound with gutta percha before assembling the bouquet.
To mount wired lily of the valley use 0.71mm (gauge 21)×36cm (14in) stubb wire according to the method shown in fig. 10. Notice that the top of the stubb wire is bent into a hook. Bind the wire and the sprig together with 0.20mm (gauge 32) silver wire and then cover the false stem with gutta percha.
Mount roses on 0.71mm (gauge 21)× 36cm (14in) stubb wire by binding with silver wire to the previously wired natural stems (fig. 11). Cover with gutta percha.
Each stephanotis has to be guttaed (ie covered with gutta percha) over existing silver wire and then re-created into sprays by binding 3 to 5 pieces onto a 0.71mm (gauge 21) stubb wire (fig. 12). Then gutta percha the spray.
Mount foliage on remaining stubb wires (fig. 10).
You should now have some 30 pieces ready for assembly.

Assembling the bouquet

Build the bouquet by starting at the bottom, which comes to a point, and working upward, broadening the design as you go. The flowers get bigger round the centre. It is easier to do this by standing and looking in a mirror.
Using 0.29mm (gauge 28) silver wire add the pieces, one at a time, binding in a circular motion (fig. 13a). As they build up, the pieces begin to form a central 'stem'. The last third of the bouquet is bent backwards (fig. 13b) to make the shape.
When all the pieces have been bound into the bouquet, trim the 'stem' to about 11cm (4½in), cover with gutta percha and tie on ribbons to complete the bouquet.

Cooking with flowers

"*Violet leaves at the entrance of Spring, fried brownish and eaten with Orange or Lemon Juice and Sugar is one of the most agreeable of the herbaceous dishes.*"

John Evelyn *Diaries* 1699

Cooking with flowers is not a mysterious art. Some of the most delicious dishes are the simplest. A bunch of roses for example, has the beauty of its rich colour, its warm, faintly spicy scent. But when the petals begin to fall, that seems to be the end of the roses' life. Yet the rose was one of the most widely used flowers in the kitchen in the past – and in fact is an excellent source of vitamin C.

The Romans put rose petals in their wine. The Persians actually made wine from the petals, and still make attar (oil) of roses today. The Bulgarians make a sweet rose liqueur, and the Chinese use liquefied roses to flavour certain pork dishes. In old recipe books, the uses for the rose seemed endless. It was made into syrups and jams, and the hips were made into tarts, marmalades and sauces. The following recipes are just a small selection of some of the most delicious examples.

Rose petal honey

12 freshly scented cabbage roses
60ml (4 tablespoons) cold water
½kg (1lb) clear honey

Remove the petals from the flower heads, discarding any that are blemished. Place them in a colander and rinse with a little cold water to make sure they are quite clean.

Put the petals in a heavy-bottomed pan. Add the 60ml (4 tablespoons) of water, and place the pan over very low heat. Stir continuously for 5 minutes.

Then pour on the honey and bring the mixture to the boil. Cover with a lid and simmer for 30 minutes. Strain off the rose petals and discard, and then pour the deliciously scented honey into a sterilized jar or pot and seal.

Rose petal syrup

Rose petal syrup is marvellous when added to soda water or cream soda, and can also be added to iced tea. It is very simple to prepare.

To make the syrup you will need:
700g (1½lb) (3 cups) closely packed
red petals
450g (1lb) (2 cups) sugar
8 cloves
600ml (1¼pints) cold water

Place all the ingredients into a heavy-bottomed pan, and bring the mixture to the boil. Reduce the heat, and sim-

mer, covered, for an hour.

Leave to cool at room temperature and strain through a fine strainer into a bowl.

Pour into a sterilized jar, and add to drinks according to taste.

Crystallized flowers

One of the most familiar ways of using flowers in the kitchen is by crystallizing the petals. Many different kinds of flowers can be used, including rose petals, *except* for plants grown from bulbs, as these will be poisonous. The most suitable varieties are violets, primroses, flowering cherry or apple blossom, and the same basic method can be used.

To make the flowers you will need:
Quantity of fresh flower heads,
picked on a dry day without any
dew on the petals.
450g (1lb) (2 cups) sugar
225ml (6fl oz) (¾ cup) water

Dissolve the sugar in the water to form a syrup, and boil it in a heavy-bottomed pan for 5 minutes. Drop the flower heads or petals into the syrup and boil for 1 minute. Using a slotted spoon, remove the petals from the syrup, and place them on a baking sheet lined with waxed paper. If necessary, separate the heads or petals and arrange them in their original shape. (A clean pair of tweezers is useful for this.) Leave the flowers in a warm dry place for 24 hours or longer until they are dry and hard, and store them in a sterilized glass jar with a tight-fitting lid.

Rose ice-cream

Once you have provided yourself with a supply of crystallized rose petals, you can use them to decorate rose ice cream, which requires no cooking at all and is quite delicious.

To make the ice cream you will need:
Block of vanilla or lemon water ice,
softened
125g (4oz) (1½ cups) red rose petals
22ml (1½ tablespoons) sugar
125ml (4fl oz) (1½ cups) red or rose
wine
A few crystallized rose petals

Wash petals gently in cold water and remove white tips at the base of the petals. Put the wine, sugar and petals into a blender, and blend until

thoroughly mixed. Alternatively, beat them together very hard with a whisk. Add the softened ice cream to the mixture and stir well. Place the mixture in the freezing compartment of the refrigerator, and leave for about eight hours, stirring gently at intervals.

A primrose flower cake is
really delicious to eat, and makes
a wonderful springtime gift
to give your friends. Notice in the
picture the jar of crystallized
violets (left) and primroses (right).

with the water, and boil for 50 minutes or until tender. Force the mixture through a strainer with the back of a wooden spoon. Stir in the sugar next and return the mixture to the pan. Boil until the mixture turns to a jelly. Allow the rose hip jelly to cool a little before spooning it into sterilized glass jars with tightly fitting lids.

Roses are lovely to cook with because they are easy to obtain, and also have large flowers. The smaller flowers of springtime such as violets and primroses, are much harder to come by. However, if you are fortunate enough to be able to obtain them, then the following recipes will make delightful eating.

Flower cake

To make the cake you will need:

6 tablespoons fresh primrose heads
6 large eggs
225g (8oz) castor (1 cup fine) sugar
150g (5oz) (1¼ cups) flour
25g (1oz) (2 tablespoons) cornflour (cornstarch)
175g (6oz) (¾ cup) clarified butter
25g (1oz) (2 tablespoons) sifted icing (confectioners') sugar

Heat the oven to 190°C (Gas Mark 5, 335°F).

Immerse the flower heads in boiling water for 1 minute, drain and set aside to drain.

Put the eggs and sugar together in a heatproof mixing bowl, and place it over a pan of simmering water. Briskly whisk the mixture until it becomes pale yellow in colour, and is the consistency of very thick cream.

Remove the bowl from the heat, and sift in half the flour, folding it in very lightly. When this is thoroughly incorporated, gradually fold in the remaining flour and the cornflour (cornstarch), a spoonful at a time, alternating with a spoonful of the clarified butter.

Finally, fold in the flower heads and pour the mixture into a 20cm (8in) square greased cake tin.

Bake the cake for 50 minutes or until it is a deep honey colour and firm to the touch.

When the cake is cool, dust it with the icing (confectioners') sugar, and serve scattered with a few fresh primroses.

Serve decorated with crystallized rose petals.

Although not strictly a flower recipe, the following rose hip conserve is an excellent way of using the fruits of the rose, with their beautiful scarlet colouring and high vitamin C content.

To make the conserve you will need:
½kg (1lb) (2 cups) hips
300ml (½pt) (1½ cups) water
½kg (1lb) (2 cups) sugar

Wash the hips, top and tail [strip] them. Place the hips in a heavy-bottomed pan

Flowers for health & beauty

"*She who on the first of May*
Goes to the fields at break of day,
And washes in the dew from the hawthorn tree,
Will ever after lovely be."

Anon. *Old Nursery Rhyme*

Before the era of manufactured cosmetics, women called upon a vast tradition of recipes derived from the natural resources of the countryside and the garden. It is common knowledge that Renaissance ladies dilated the pupils of their eyes with Belladonna to achieve a mysterious, limpid effect, and that Elizabeth I of England whitened her face with powder. However, as well as extremes of fashion such as these, there are many recipes which are still useful for skin and hair care, even for today's city based woman. Flower waters made from lavender and roses are, of course, still commercially made, but it is fun to learn how to make them up at home.

The basic processes

Two very basic processes are very useful as a foundation for using flowers as beauty aids. They are both methods of extracting the essence of the flowers – one by infusing the petals in water, and the other by soaking them in oil. Both are useful to know, for then the essences can be used in a variety of different ways.

Infusion in water

An infusion is made by pouring boiling water over the flower petals or heads. The usual proportions are 3 teaspoons of the flowers to 250ml (8fl oz) (1 cup) of water. You may like to increase the amount of petals depending upon the strength of their perfume. Make infusions of the following varieties of flowers – roses, lavender, verbena, lily of the valley, geranium, tuberose, lime, violets, elder and chamomile flowers, and use the resulting liquid as colognes. They can be added to the bath, and remember that the chamomile infusion is an excellent hair rinse for fair hair, while the elder water refreshes tired eyes at the end of the day.

As well as being good for the eyes, elder flower water is traditionally effective as a way of taking away freckles, while the lime flower infusion reputedly smooths away wrinkles, and can also be used as a hair rinse. If you are feeling really extravagent, run a hot bath, and sprinkle handfuls of your favourite scented petals into the water, and leave it to 'infuse' on a grand scale. You may not be feeling so happy when the time comes to retrieve the soggy petals from the bathtub so

perhaps a wiser policy would be to put your flowers into a muslin bag, and suspend it beneath the hot tap of the bath. If you just need to revive your aching feet, try an infusion of lime or marigold flowers in a footbath.

Flower oils

The one drawback involved in this method of extracting the essence of flowers is the amount of blossoms needed. However, if you are fortunate enough to have an abundant supply of flowers, then do try this method. The

best oils to use for this purpose are almond, avocado, sunflower, safflower, sesame seed and olive oil. Remember that olive oil has a strong smell of its

own, so if you dislike the perfume, choose one like almond oil. You can use the same kinds of flowers as those mentioned above for infusions. For a generous amount of essence, pour 600ml (1pt) (2½ cups) of the oil into a bowl, and put in as many fresh flowers as the oil will take and cover. Let the flowers soak for two days in the covered bowl and keep in a warm place.

Remove them, strain out and squeeze the wilted blossoms, and then add as many fresh flowers to the oil as you can. Leave again for two days, strain and squeeze out the flowers, and repeat this process with about ten batches of blossoms. During the soaking, always keep the bowl covered.

Finally strain the oil, and store in tightly capped or corked bottles. Use as regular bath oils.

Cosmetic vinegars

A really old-fashioned way of preparing flowers for cosmetic use was to soak them in vinegar. Use a good brand of white wine vinegar, and steep a good handful of the flowers in a jar which is tightly covered, and leave the mixture to infuse on a sunny shelf. Use in the bath as a really refreshing tonic. If you have made your vinegar from rose petals, it is excellent as a skin toner.

Creams and face packs

One way of using your flower oils is to make your own luxury face cream. Any plain unscented cold cream is suitable as a base. Heat the cold cream very gently in a pan, and add to it a few precious drops of your flower oil.

Alternatively, you may like to try a face pack, based on yoghurt. Chop up some elderflowers, or lime flowers, mix them with the yoghurt, and spread the mixture evenly over the face, avoiding the eyes and mouth. Leave on for 10–15 minutes, and then wash off with lukewarm water.

Another type of face pack can be made by mixing elder flowers or marigolds with honey. Use as above.

Sometimes skin becomes sore and blemished, perhaps from sun or wind burn, or because of acne. Do remember that as well as applying cosmetics to your skin, a sensible diet is also very important. Some of the infusions of flowers and hot water can be drunk as teas – those made with chamomile or lime flowers are traditionally reputed to maintain a healthy digestion, and act as an overall tonic. However, if you have a problem with sore skin, the following elderflower cream has excellent healing qualities.

Elderflower cream

Gather enough elderflowers to fill a 450g (1lb) (2 cups) jar, and add 15g (½oz) of white wax (available from pharmacies). Next add 250ml (8fl oz) (1 cup) of almond oil. Place the jar in a pan of water, bring the water to the boil, and stir the mixture from time to time. Let it simmer for half an hour, and leave to cool. Strain off the petals and store in clean airtight containers.

Soaking petals to extract their essence is a very old process.

Dried & pressed flowers

"*Gather ye rosebuds while ye may,*
Old Time is still a-flying:
And this same flower that smiles today,
To-morrow will be dying."

Robert Herrick *Hesperides* 1591-1674

CALENDAR

How to dry flowers

There are three basic ways of preserving plant material such as flowers, foliage, seed heads, leaves and grasses. Try them all if you can. If you can't, choose the method most suited to the facilities that you have available.

If, for example, you have an airy space with room for hooks or a line to hang the flowers on, you can try air drying. Flowers dried out by the second method – in a dessicant powder such as borax or silica gel – may be easier for some in that the only space required is a large box to hold the powder and the flowers.

Plant material can also be preserved with glycerine; the main requirements are some jars, bottles and the space to store them upright.

Details for each of these methods are given below, but before you begin preserving flowers you must know when to pick them so they will be in the best possible condition to give the best results. Also, some plants are more suited to one method of preservation than to others.

Gathering flowers

Try to cut the flowers on a dry, warm day when there will be a minimum of moisture on the plant surface. Never pick material when it is raining or when dew is forming. As a general rule, choose flowers just before they come into full bloom. Fully open blossoms, or flowers that have already begun to set seed, will merely shed petals and seeds as you attempt to preserve them.

Air drying

Pick the material and remove the leaves from the stems. Leaves that are left on will simply wither and tangle in the stems as they are drying.

If the flowers are fairly small, put them into small bunches and tie them with

Many flowers can be preserved by simply hanging them upside down in a cool, dry dark place such as a cupboard.

string or plastic ties, leaving a loop to slide onto a line or hook.

If you have chosen material with large flower heads, try to hang them separately. There is nothing more frustrating than to dry flowers perfectly and then to damage them in trying to disentangle the florets. As the material dries it will tend to shrink, so you may need to tighten the ties to hold the stems securely.

The bunches must be hung, well apart, on a line or on hooks in a cool, dry, airy and dark place. Too much light and warmth tend to make the material brittle and faded, and flowers become mildewed in damp surroundings.

Drying upright

Flowers with heavy or fragile heads can be dried by standing them upright in a jar. For this method make sure that the plant has a strong stem and that the head does not tend to droop. If the stems are very short, cut down to about 2.5cm (1in) from the head and push a length of 0.9mm (19–20 gauge) florists' wire up the stem and into the flower head and push the end of the wire into a bed of sand or a piece of plastic foam. Leave the flowers to dry in this position.

How long to dry?

The length of drying time necessary varies enormously. Delicate material such as grasses may only take a week, but heavier flowers, containing more moisture, may need three weeks or more.
The material should be checked to see if it feels quite dry and dehydrated before removing it for storage. Hydrangea and molucella, both very popular in dried flower arrangements, require a little extra attention. The plants should be cut and stripped of leaves as usual. The stems should then be placed in about 5cm (2in) of water and left in a warm room. When all the water has gone the stems should be tied, hung and left to dry as usual. (Cut hydrangeas on a new stem if possible.)

Below: Drying flowers in powder—
1. Pour dessicant powder into box.
2. Place blossoms carefully
into the powder.
3. Cover the flowers completely.

Suitable flowers

This list of plants is very far from being complete, but it is a guide to suitable material. If you would like to try drying a flower that is not included then there is nothing to lose in experimenting to see if it will work.
The following three flowers are often used in dried arrangements and are called everlastings: ammobium alatum grandiflorum (everlasting sand flower) has silvery-white petals and a domed yellow centre. It grows to about 0.6m (2ft) tall but the stems are short in proportion to the flower heads, so you may need to lengthen them when you come to arrange them; anaphalis (pearl ever-lasting) which has a grey leaf and a white flower and helichrysum bracteatum (straw flower) which has flowers rather like those of a stiff, shiny-petalled double daisy in an assortment of colours. This must be cut before the flowers are fully open.
Other rounded shapes are achillea filipendulina (garden yarrow) – dry by standing in an empty jar to avoid damaging the large flower heads; and catananche caerulea (cupid's dart).
Spiky shapes which can be air dried are acanthus spinosus (bear's breeches), useful for large arrangements; delphinium (pick as soon as the top floret opens, and dry hanging upside down), and limonium sinuatum (sea lavender).

Drying clusters

Clusters which are effective in dried arrangements are acacia dealbata (mimosa) – the little yellow balls remain and hold some of their perfume; eryingium (sea holly) – cut before the seed heads mature; and gypsolphila elegans (baby's breath).
Leaves and grasses include aspidistra (parlour palm); briza maxima (pearl

grass) and lagurus ovatus (hare's tail).

Seeds, fruits and cones

Seedheads include alliums (dry upside down if possible); aquilegia (columbine); dipsacus fullonium (teasels); and lunaria (honesty).
Fruits and cones can be opened by drying in a cool oven while cucurbita (gourds) should be ripened by hanging them up by the stems or by placing them on a tray and turning frequently.

Drying flowers in powder

The powders used in this method are borax, silica gel crystals, or sand, and of these silica gel is probably the best. It dries flowers efficiently and the crystals are very light and therefore less likely to crush delicate blossoms. Furthermore, silica gel crystals can be dried out in a warm oven after use and then used again. Both silica gel and borax can be bought in pharmacies.
The advantage of drying in powder is that flowers preserved by this method retain much of their original colour. Some silica gel preparations on the market, (there are several brands), have additional chemicals which help retain vivid hues to a truly amazing degree. But these flowers are susceptible to damp and if your room is not fairly dry they should be kept under glass. Before beginning to use a dessicant powder, the flowers must be dry and in good condition. Any of the powders may be used, although sand tends to be rather heavy for delicate petals.

Method of drying
Cover the bottom of a box or biscuit tin with the powder, carefully lay the flowers on this and pour over more powder (fig. 1) so they are completely

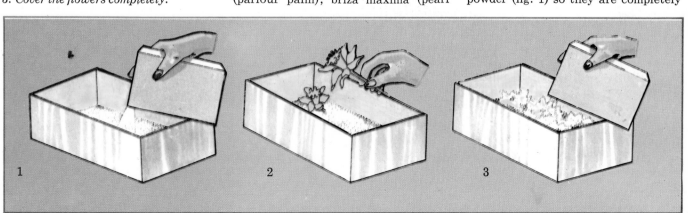

1 2 3

Powder, wire, tape and foam all help to create beautiful arrangements.

covered. Take care that there is plenty of powder between the petals and stamens. Leave them, and the powder will draw the moisture from the petals. Make sure that you do not add any moisture to the mixture by putting the box in a damp place. The box should be kept in a warm, dry place.

The length of time it takes to dry the flowers again varies. To test, gently scrape off powder from a petal; if any trace of moisture remains, re-cover and leave. Most flowers take about two days to dry completely.

When they are dry, remove and store them in a dark place. You could store them in a box, adding a few crystals of silica gel to absorb any moisture. Florists' wire to support the stems can be added before or after drying.

Choosing flowers

This method is more suited to flowers than foliage. The more simple and open-faced flowers are best – anemones, marigolds, daisies and cornflowers, for example. Small roses can be very successful if you make quite sure that the powder is well distributed among the petals. Larger specimens tend to work less well with this method.

Preserving in glycerine

This process replaces the water in the plant with glycerine, giving a supple and quite lasting result. Glycerine looks like a clear, syrupy liquid.

Stems should be placed in water for a

48

few hours before putting them in the glycerine. Make sure that the material is in good condition before you begin – attempting to preserve damaged leaves is a waste of effort. Woody stems should be split to make sure that the glycerine can travel up them.

Glycerine method

Make a mixture of two-parts water to one-part glycerine and place the stems in about 10cm (4in) of the liquid. Leave for about two or three weeks when the leaves should become supple and change colour. Remove from the glycerine mixture and, if the leaves begin to droop, hang them upside down for a few days to make sure that the glycerine reaches to the top.
Plant material to be preserved by this method should be gathered before the dying autumn colours begin to show – if you leave it too late, the plant loses its power to absorb liquid.

Suitable flowers for glycerine preserving

These include clematis vitalba (wild clematis) – the flower heads do not disintegrate and the leaves turn deep

bronze; hydrangea; molucella laevis (bells of Ireland) – preserve these in a dry place to avoid mould. The mixture may not be able to reach the upper flowers, so it is helpful to remove a few top flowers before you begin; polygonatum multiflorum (Solomon's Seal).
The glycerine method is particularly

Below left: Leaves and foliage can be preserved by using glycerine.

Below: Arrangement under glass.

suitable for leaves – here is a brief list of some of the possibilities: Aspidistra lurida (parlour palm) – process may take up to six months; convallaria majalis (lily of the valley) – leaves may be completely submerged in the mixture; fagus sylvatica (beech) – pick while still green and fresh.
Beech nuts left on the branch will also be preserved; helleborus (Christmas Rose); magnoloa grandiflora (magnolia); quercus (oak); and rhododendron all preserve successfully.

Arranging dried flowers

Dried flower arrangements can be approached in much the same way as fresh flower arrangements – but there are some advantages. Since dried flowers do not require water, it is not necessary for all the stems to stand in a vase – other supports can be used. Also, they are more obedient to the arranger and will not twist and droop in an arrangement. Best of all, dried arrangements are everlasting and so make splendid decorations all year around, especially in the winter when fresh flowers are hard to get and very expensive for regular arranging.

Preparing the material

Before you begin an arrangement, some of the dried plant material may require extra care. Dried flowers and grasses can be bought from time to time in florist shops. Florist's stubb wires should be used for making false stems when necessary. The thickness of the wire used depends on the material and its purpose. Gauges 0.90mm, 0.71mm and 0.56mm are the most commonly used. Delicate leaves can be reinforced with silver reel wire, and wire stems concealed with florist's tape (gutta percha). These are available from floral supply houses or can sometimes be purchased from your local florist shop. A hollow corn stalk can be slipped over the wire to conceal it too.

It will help to preserve delicate seedheads if you spray them with hair lacquer before arranging them, and many berries can be preserved by brushing them with a mixture of $\frac{1}{2}$ clear shellac and $\frac{1}{2}$ alcohol. Leave them in an airy place to dry.

Supports in the container

The most commonly used support for dried and fresh flowers is crumpled wire mesh with 5cm (2in) gaps. This does not always produce a close enough texture, however, to hold the fine wire stems on some dried material.

Florist's foam (used dry), and blocks of dry foam which are made especially for dried arrangements, are alternatives. As the foam is light and will overbalance easily it must be anchored to the container. This can be done by impaling it on a pin holder, by covering it with wire mesh and securing the mesh to the container with a wire, or by wrapping a weight into the base of the foam.

Plasticine can also be used. A lump of this should be pressed firmly into the base of a dry, clean container, and the stems pushed into it. Plaster of Paris may be used in the same way provided you can make up your arrangement before it sets hard. In both methods it is easier to see what you are doing if you use a shallow container.

Glaring white plastic can be concealed by painting it or rubbing it with brown shoe polish when it is quite dry.

Containers

There are no hard and fast rules about what containers to use for dried arrangements. Glass containers would obviously be unsuitable if you have lots of foam and underpinnings to conceal, but gently curving, golden stems of corn would add to the grace of an arrangement.

Because the containers do not need to be watertight, rush or wicker baskets can be used. A flat wooden slab makes an excellent base, using well-disguised plasticine as a support. Smaller arrangements can be made to fit snugly into a scallop shell or a candlestick. Candles themselves look pretty surrounded by dried flowers, but be very careful to keep the dried material well away from the flame as it is highly inflammable.

Arranging the material

It is most likely that if you care enough about flowers to make the effort to select and preserve them, you will also have a feeling for making them look attractive in an arrangement.
Assuming you have chosen a container

Either choose flowers of the same kind (left) or create a wildly fanciful extravaganza of colour in a massed arrangement such as this one (right) by David Hicks.

and have the necessary supports firmly in place, then the next step is to arrange your material.

A good rule is to have different quantities of the various flowers or leaves. Even quantities tend to make monotonous displays and the last thing you want is a 'stagey' effect.

Types of arrangements

Dried flowers are as versatile as fresh. Your arrangements can be as delicate or as elaborate as you wish – a few wispy flowers in muted tones on a coffee table make an effective 'shape', or a straightforward, formal arrangement, made very much as though you were working with fresh flowers and bearing in mind each flower's contribution to the whole arrangement. Alternatively you can make a fabulous, massed con-

coction. By adding new sprigs, even green ones, and letting them dry in the arrangement, it becomes an ever-growing one. This kind of arrangement is entirely dependent on your materials, how much space there is in the room and the size of your container. For the more traditional arrangement, how-ever, you need to follow a basic building procedure.

Formal arrangements

Formal arrangements need a basic outline, focal interest and filling material. The first step is to place the tall outline material. Place the first three pieces to fix the outline points – make the three points of a triangle, for example, with the stems coming from a central point. To give depth to the arrangement, avoid putting the outline points on the same plane.

The items which make up the focal points of the arrangement should be placed near the middle and fairly low in the overall pattern. Don't make this part so strong that it kills the rest of the material to make the arrangement come to life. Hydrangea or clusters of vivid berries would be a good choice for this position.

The procedures used for arranging dried flowers are very much the same as for fresh. Figs. a and b illustrate the classic triangular shape on which the arrangement (left) is based. Tall outline material is used first, then the larger flowers are added in the centre. The arrangement below is much more informal and simple in approach.

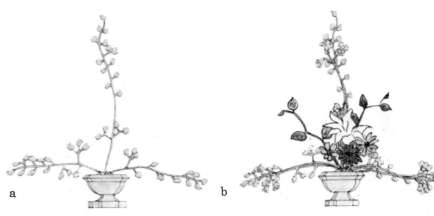

a   b

53

Using filler material

Filler material – grasses for example – should be used to blend the focal interest points with the outline material. The aim is not to fill in all the remaining gaps but to make the whole arrangement harmonize. This is a dangerous stage in the arrangement, when it is very tempting to go on adding more and more material. Stop when you see that there is enough material to complete a graceful design.

Re-working

Dried flowers can be re-worked indefinitely in arrangements of different sizes, combinations and shapes, provided they are treated with special care. Some are, of course, more brittle than others, and all are liable to break. It is not usual, however, to keep on using the same flowers in different arrangements for years, and they can be stored away in the attic or cupboard when not in use, eg during the summer when the scents and hues of freshly cut flowers make them an irresistible pleasure to bring to the home.

If you are careful to blend the colours well, you can mix dried flowers with artificial ones.

Pressing flowers

One of the joys of working with pressed flowers is that it enables you to produce the most delicate designs without being able to draw. Instead of draughtsmanship the qualities required are neat fingers, patience and a love of plants. The natural beauty of the flowers makes them a perfect material for creating a work of art.

Suitable flowers

The best flowers for pressing are simple ones. Those with too many large petals, a prominent seed area or a thick bulky stem are too clumsy to press well.

Common but insignificant wild flowers can look beautiful when pressed and are invaluable for decoration. Buttercups and daisies are easy to press. Daisy stems are useful for adding to flowers which have stems unsuitable for pressing, either because they are damaged or they do not suit the design. The stems of plants such as the primrose, clover and clematis are other useful substitutes.

When choosing specimens bear in mind the line and curve of the whole flower, as this is important in an arrangement. Dog violet, for example, has a gracefully curved stem. Larger varieties such as delphinium, hydrangea or azalea can only be used successfully if the individual florets are picked off and pressed separately. You will find there is ample scope for experimentation both in the type of flowers you press and the time it takes to press them.

Leaves and grasses

Leaves, grasses, sedges and ferns are as important to collect as the flowers themselves. Apart from often being very delicate they give texture to an arrangement. They are usually picked when young and before the seeds have formed.

If the leaves look too large for the flower, try to find a smaller leaf from a seedling. Ivy leaves are very decorative as is the brilliantly hued autumn foliage of prunus or Virginia creeper. You can obtain an attractive contrast by turning a pressed leaf to display its underside.

Picking for pressing

Flowers should be picked with scissors or secateurs so as to avoid pulling up roots accidentally. Pick your material under the best possible conditions. Given three or four days of fine, dry weather, you can continue to collect your plant material as long as conditions last. It is important that floral material should be obtained as dry as possible in order to give satisfactory results. If flowers are the slightest bit damp when pressed they will lose their colour or go mouldy. Only pick perfect specimens.

When to press

Flowers should be pressed as soon as possible after picking. Wild flowers wilt especially quickly. Collect the flowers and put them in a plastic

Pressing flowers is a delicate task to undertake, but the results are well worthwhile. You can create lovely pressed pictures like this.

bag and close it securely with a rubber band. Do not gather too many flowers or they will crush each other. Never put flowers in water once they have been picked or leave them in the bag longer than a couple of hours as the condensation created in the bag will ruin the material.

Temporary press

If you are away from home, take a simple home-made press with you. Make this from two rectangles of cardboard, about 35cm×43cm (14in×17in), held together with two rubber bands. Lay out the flowers between sheets of newspaper or blotting paper cut the same size as the press and place the sheets between the two rectangles of cardboard. Secure with the rubber bands. This will give temporary and satisfactory results until you return home.

Pressing methods

Flowers can be pressed in various ways for an interesting variety of results. Pressing can be done in books. Place the flowers carefully between the pages of a thick book made of absorbent, not shiny, paper. Do not use your best coffee table volumes, instead obtain some old wallpaper pattern books or telephone directories.

You will need:
Books for pressing.
Cardboard name tags and felt-tipped pens for labelling.
Weights such as bricks.

Sort your flowers and leaves into similar groups for easy access when designing your pictures, cards, lamp-shades etc. Press flowers of the same thickness next to each other so that they receive the same amount of pressure as each other.
Common wild flowers can be pressed complete with stems and leaves. Butter-cups and daisies could even have their heads turned to one side.
Individual florets such as those of a primula or delphinium should be snipped off their stems.
Petals of flowers with hard centres should be gently pulled off for pressing. They can be reassembled for your designs with a centre from a different flower if necessary.
Press as many flowers as will com-

fortably fit on one page without touching each other.
Insert a name tag with details of pressing date and colour of flower (fig. 1). Leave several pages of your pressing book between every layer of flowers.
Place heavy weights such as bricks on the book and leave undisturbed in a dry, well-aired room for four weeks.

1

Making a press

A flower press can be bought from a craft shop or you can make your own. You can experiment with substitute presses such as two pieces of wood or hardboard or sheets of corrugated cardboard held together with elastic.

You will need:
A press.
Blotting paper, newspaper or tea towel.
Layer of corrugated paper (optional).

Sandwich your plant material between blotting paper, newspaper or tea towel cut to fit between the four bolts. To press several layers use corrugated paper between each layer. Insert the bolts and tighten the butterfly screws to apply pressure. Check the pressing at least every other day. Some flowers contain more moisture and if blotting paper or cloth is damp it must be changed for a fresh layer.

Wood and hardboard

Lilies, tulips and similarly-formed flowers need to be pressed between wood or hardboard. Cut several strips of cardboard about 2cm×7.5cm (¾in× 3in). Gently open out the first petal of the flower, working from left to right. Place a thin cardboard strip over the petal and secure each end to the wood or hardboard with adhesive tape. Repeat this until the entire flower is covered (see fig. 2). Daffodils can be pressed like this if the trumpets are

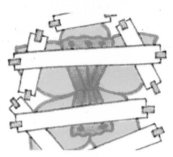

2

slit in half vertically. Place the second piece of wood or hardboard on top and secure with rubber bands.

Drying time
Drying time for all the methods described depends on the condition of the flowers, the outdoor weather conditions and the temperature in the room in which the material is drying. This can vary from four weeks to a few days.

Storing pressed flowers
Store your pressed material in used kitchen containers such as margarine tubs, transparent-top cheese boxes or clear plastic sandwich containers so that the contents, which should be stored in colours, shapes and species, can easily be seen. Material can also be kept in plastic bags.

Make a press by drilling holes in wood with 1cm (⅜in) bit. Connect pieces with four 1cm (⅜in) diameter bolts, 10cm (4in) long with matching washers and butterfly screws.

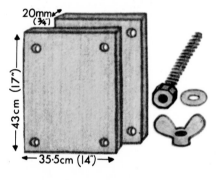

The above illustrations show only a few of the possibilities for making patterns with pressed flowers. Experiment with a variety of combinations until you're happy.

Decorating with pressed flowers

Pressed flowers and plant materials have many imaginative and often unconventional uses, all of which involve decorative design. Once you have acquired a selection of pressed flowers and leaves, you can begin to design with them. Undoubtedly, the most popular surface for pressed flower designs is paper, and decorating notepaper or greetings cards make good projects for beginners.

The most challenging and rewarding enterprise, however, is designing and making pressed flower pictures. Pressed material can be used to mimic natural history prints or flower paintings. Petals can be stuck down singly to re-build a particular flower or to create collages and abstract patterns. Grasses can be pasted down to re-create whole fields and trees and, if framing is properly planned, surfaces can also be built out to give depth to a picture.

Designs need not be confined to pictures. Wood, plastic, and other surfaces can all be decorated with pressed flower and plant material.

Planning a design

Completely straight lines rarely occur in nature and this is a principle to remember when you are planning a design. Observe the formations of plants as they grow and try to echo these in your designs.

Proportion is very important. Keep your flowers in scale with the object you are decorating. The tiniest wild flower can look delightful on a bookmark yet fade into insignificance on a larger piece of work.

Using colour

Colour changes are inevitable in some flowers when they are pressed and these can be exploited by cleverly blending and contrasting them. Cream-coloured flowers, such as lily of the valley, fade to a browny shade in time. Some, such as broom and dog myrtle, turn black. Blues may fade a little, although dark

blue delphiniums and larkspur will retain their colour well. Bright reds tend to darken to a chocolate colour. Celandines, after a year or so, turn a beautiful silvery white.

To help preserve the colours of your flowers, never display them in a too-sunny position.

Damaged material need not be discarded. If some petals of a flower have pressed badly, use them for filling in backgrounds or incorporate the good pieces into another flower.

Floral pictures such as the one opposite, and decorating household items with pressed leaves are good ways of using the art creatively.

Choosing backgrounds

Backgrounds should be chosen which enhance the subtle tones of pressed flowers and leaves. Avoid indefinite neutral beiges. Instead, use clear white, black or a positive colour.

Start designing your first projects with a small scale effort. You can make greetings cards, place cards or gift tags by adding a simple spray of flowers and leaves. If you have difficulty in the first arrangements you can adapt ideas from commercial greetings cards. Try tossing a handful of pressed flower heads at random on a card, then sticking them down.

Sticking down flowers

Before actually sticking down the

Pamela McDowall. 7.11.70

You can either have a very definite shape in mind, like this floral butterfly, or else use some flowers as a focal point, and build up the design from there (left).

flowers it is wisest to work out your design of a flat surface. Once glued you can easily ruin your plant material by trying to remove and reposition it. Decide on which surface to decorate. Matchboxes, birthday cards, paper lampshades or wooden wall plaques all lend themselves to pressed flower designs.

Where the surface to be decorated is not already a plain colour (such as a matchbox), cut a piece of stiff paper or cardboard to fit the surface you are decorating, stick it down and fix your plant material to that. Having selected the plant material you will be using for the design, pick it up and position it with a pair of tweezers.

Experiment

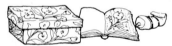

Now is the time to experiment and reposition the material till you are satisfied with your design.

If you are designing on cardboard or fabric use a latex-based adhesive.

For a wood surface use a clear glue. Apply a spot of adhesive on the corolla of a whole flower, on the top end of single petals or on the centres of smaller leaves. Grasses and stems need only be stuck down at one or two points.

Use the tip of a screwdriver to apply the adhesive and press down with the end of the handle. Any excess latex adhesive can be removed easily by rubbing it off with your finger. This will leave no stain on the paper. Wipe off any excess clear glue before it has had time to dry. Always use the adhesive or glue very sparingly. Leave the work•

overnight to allow the adhesive to dry thoroughly.

Surface protection

It is advisable to protect your material from constant handling and dust. This can be done by various means:

Self-adhesive plastic can be used for small decorations on matchboxes, notebooks or bookmarks.

Place the self-adhesive plastic film over the arrangement. Starting at one corner, peel off the backing a little at a time. With your other hand gently smooth the film into position taking care to avoid air bubbles. Once the plastic is in position it cannot be moved without damaging the arrangement so place it carefully.

Finish by trimming away the surplus plastic with sharp scissors.

Using varnishes

Polyurethane transparent varnish can be used effectively to cover pressed flowers on wooden surfaces. The technique is similar to découpage where paper cut-outs are stuck to a prepared surface which is then covered with many layers of clear varnish. Pressed flowers can be used in this way to decorate boxes, wall plaques or jewellery. (Use wood with an attractive texture and grain and it will not need staining.)

Prepare the surface by sanding lightly

and then removing dust.

Apply a thin coat of polyurethane varnish to the wood and smooth the surface again with sandpaper.

Attach the flowers and leaves firmly with adhesive as described previously so that they do not move about under the brush when applying varnish. Leave to dry overnight.

How to prevent fading

To prevent the flowers fading under varnish you must 'cheat' by touching them up with a little water-colour paint. As the water-colour paint is likely to run off the pressed material without adhering to it, dip your paintbrush into a little liquid detergent before applying the paint. This will keep the paint from running onto the decorated surface by making the plant material more absorbent.

Gloss, semi-gloss or matt varnish can be used to cover the flowers. Many layers may be necessary on thick-stemmed material before the surface is sufficiently smooth to the touch. Finish with very fine sandpaper and steel wool, using a circular movement.

Remove any particles from the surface with a damp cloth and give a final polish with an old nylon stocking rolled into a ball.

Glass is ideal for covering and protecting pressed flower arrangements on trays, tabletops and pictures.

Making a picture

You can create a simple flower design or build up your plant material to make a scene. A leaf could form the roof of a house, grasses can be used as tree-

Pressed flowers make enchanting designs for table mats (above) and are also ideal for making greetings cards such as the ones below.

trunks and branches. With a little imagination you could devise all sorts of interesting scenes. Background can be either of white or coloured paper or fabric such as velvet, linen or silk.

You will need
Pressed flower material.
Frame, glass and hardboard backing.
Paper or fabric for background.
Tweezers, screwdriver, scissors.
Latex adhesive.
Soft baby's hairbrush.
Hammer, panel pins, hooks and cord for hanging picture.

Remove glass from frame and keep to one side.
Prepare background, either cutting backing cardboard to size or carefully sticking fabric to hardboard backing. An overlap is unnecessary as the edges will be covered by the frame. (Leave a margin for the frame when arranging your design.)
When building up the design select two or three special flowers as focal points, then fill in with smaller details. Use adhesive sparingly.
Use a soft hairbrush to remove any particles of dust from the background.
Replace glass and finish frame in the usual way.

Making pot pourri

The fragrances of sweet-smelling herbs, spices and flowers can be captured all year round in pot-pourri and sachets. Rooms, cupboards, household and personal linen can be kept fragrant and fresh with all the varieties of aromatic plants. You can give each drawer or cupboard a distinctive scent – sweet, spicy, delicate or intoxicating – making it both a special pleasure to open it and the contents delightful to wear or use in the home.

Fragrant herbs and flowers grow everywhere. They can be gathered and dried or they can be bought already dried at herbalist shops and mixed at home with essential oils and fixatives to give them scent. It is in the subtle blending of these fragrances and, in pot-pourri, of colour, too, that herbal art lies.

Harvesting

Spring and summer are the seasons to harvest herbs and flowers for sweet-smelling pot-pourri, sachets and herb pillows, for once winter comes most of the herbs varnish from sight.

You must harvest herbs when their aromatic oils are most powerful, so pick them just before they flower, in the early morning when the dew has dried and before the sun is hot. Pick flowers when they are just open and absolutely unblemished, even though it seems hard to plunder them at that moment.

Harvest seeds when they are ready to fall, and roots at the end of the season. Pick only enough to lightly cover whatever drying shelves you have arranged and let the leaves remain on the stem. Separate any petals you want. Handle both leaves and flowers very gently to prevent bruising. As you pick herbs or flowers lay them one-deep on a tray or flat box.

Drying herbs and flowers

Your aim is to dry the herbs quite quickly with an even, low warmth – not less than 70°F (21°C) or more than 100°F (38°C). A good, even ventilation is just as important as the heat to carry away the humidity of the drying plants. Too much heat or too sunny or light a place will brown the leaves or, at least, dissipate the aromatic properties you are trying to conserve. So you want a dark place with little or no dust, but warmth and plenty of air.

Where to dry

Possible drying places are an airing cupboard or a clothes drying cupboard; a plate-warming compartment of a stove; a darkened, warm, well-ventilated room, passage or cupboard where you could set up a small fan heater; an attic, garage or darkened green-house; a dry, well-aired cellar, perhaps near a boiler.

The shelves must be well separated so

Dried herbs and pot pourri make lovely gifts, either packed into transparent boxes or as sachets. A luxurious container of pot pourri (right) perfumes the entire room.

All the heady fragrances of a luscious summer garden can be brought together with herbs and spices to provide the ingredients for a classic pot pourri.

that air can pass freely between them. You could use muslin tacked to a wooden framework, hessian [burlap] or any open weave cloth stretched over dowels or framing, or the flat bottoms of cardboard boxes which have been perforated to let air through, but do not use wire mesh.

If you can alter and regulate the heat, one method is to begin drying with a temperature of about 90°F (32°C) for one day and then reduce the heat to 70°F (21°C) until the drying process is finished.

The drying space should only faintly smell of herbs; a strong smell means there is too much heat and escaping aromas. Don't add a fresh batch of herbs until the first batch is dry or you will add more humidity to the air. Turn the herbs as they are drying from time to time.

Experiment with drying until you get the fullest colour and smell in the herbs. It takes from four to 14 days or more to dry herbs, and flowers are better dried slowly at a lower temperature than herbs.

Leaves are dry when they are brittle but will not shatter. Flower petals should feel dry and slightly crisp. Roots should dry right through with no soft centre.

Store all dried plants in airtight containers in a cool, dark place.

Air drying

Tying a bunch of herbs and flowers and hanging them upside down in a dry airy space is an old method of drying herbs, and more satisfactory in a dry climate than in a humid one. Air drying is likely to retain less colour and scent but needs no special arrangements.

Pot-pourri

Pot-pourri can be made of all scented plants – flowers, fruits, herbs, barks, spices – and it is the blending of these that produces the dimly fragrant, sometimes mysterious, aromas.

Choose a main scent – it is often rose petals in a pot-pourri, lavender in a sachet – then add others to give the

mixture fleeting undertones. You can also add drops of essential oils bought from a herb stockist. A fixative, such as orris root, is needed to hold the perfumes longer than the flowers and leaves can on their own.

Choosing a container
Choose a beautiful container – an apothecary jar, open-work silver or ceramic pot, china or porcelain box or urn. If the pot-pourri is to be seen, arrange it with leaves of elusive greens, small rosebuds, marigolds, pressed violets, pansies and everlasting flowers. Some of these do not hold their scent as well as, say, roses, tuberoses and lavender, but they give perfect shape and delicate colour.

Experimenting with scents
Experiments with scents because they vary from garden to garden and overlap from plant to plant. For example, neroli is a scented substance in fragrant roses which is also in geraniums, jasmine, orange blossom and wallflowers. Citronellol is in roses, geraniums and eucalyptus, and eugenol is in bay, cloves, hyacinths and tuberoses. The choice of scent is infinite – violet, jonquil, narcissus, lilac, honeysuckle, lily of the valley, the mints, rose geranium, rosemary, and in warmer climates, oleander, magnolia, lotus, jasmine, gardenia, orange blossom, acacia or wattles.

Also consider using these – cloves, nutmeg, cinnamon, mace, vanilla pod from the Mexican creeper, woodruff, tonquin beans, sandalwood, cedar and sassafras, eucalyptus leaves and citrus peel from oranges and lemons.

Floral pot-pourri

There are dozens of combinations to experiment with, but this one is simple.
1 lit (2pt) rose petals.
0.5 lit (1pt) rose geranium leaves.
0.5 lit (1pt) lavender flowers.
1 cup rosemary needles.
2 tablespoons each of ground cloves, cinnamon, allspice.
3 tablespoons crushed orris root and powdered gum benzoin.
20 drops essential oil of rose.
5 drops essential oil of sandalwood or citrus.

Jasmine pot-pourri.
0.5 lit (1pt) jasmine flowers.
0.3 lit (½pt) orange blossoms and gardenias.
0.3 lit (½pt) geranium leaves, including the lemon, peppermint and rose-scented ones.

57gm (2oz) cassia.
57gm (2oz) gum benzoin.
A vanilla pod of drops of vanilla oil.

Add drops of oils to dried flowers and fixatives, then put flowers, leaves and spices in layers in the container. Use small, whole flowers and leaves to decorate the top layer. Place mixture in airtight container and leave jar for six weeks, turning contents weekly.

Herb pillows

For dreams of summer, put a herb pillow in your pillow case. Herbs to sooth the insomniac include angelica, woodruff, sage, hops, dill, camomile, bergamot, lavender, valerian (a rather unpleasant smell), lemon balm, lemon verbena, tarragon, elder flowers and borage.

The herbs that were used for strewing on bare floors in the Middle Ages are also good for herb pillows – thyme, mint, basil, hyssop, marjaram and rosemary.

Make a cotton or muslin bag to any size you want, to hold the herbs, and then make a cover for it that can be laundered – in sprigged cotton or perhaps white embroidery on white cotton. Mix together equal parts of lavender, lemon verbena and mint, and add small quantities of any herbs listed above.

Or mix equal parts of rosemary blossoms, rosemary needles, pine needles, rose geranium leaves and lemon balm. Or mix equal parts of rose petals and lavender, and add small amounts of woodruff, camomile, dill, sage, bergamot and tarragon.

Or use hops only. Many people feel a hop pillow is best for insomnia.

Sachets

Hang these on hangers; put them in drawers, linen cupboards and under cushions. Try a half-and-half mixture of lavender and lemon verbena; or southernwood, bergamot and lemon balm with twice as many rose petals and lavender.

If you wish, add to any of these mixtures some spices – coriander seeds, cloves or cinnamon.

Sachets can be made of small squares of silk, cotton print or organdie, and treated as miniature pillows, or they can be gathered across the top and secured with a ribbon. This method means that they can be refilled later on.

Lavender cushions

This pretty selection of lavender cushions has a general theme in terms of colour but variety is achieved with the use of different, lightweight fabrics. Each completed cushion measures about 7cm (3in) square, except for the gathered-up sachets, which are rectangular in shape. (If you choose a fabric with an open weave you will also need lining fabric.)

Cut out a back and front from the fabric, with a small seam allowance on each side.

Embroider fabric with cross stitch, satin stitch, leaf or running stitch in contrasting threads. Alternatively, sew on trimmings such as lace or ric-rac.

With right sides facing, sew the two pieces together leaving one side open. Turn sachet right side out and fill with lavender. Whip stitch open side seams together.

Note that the gathered-up sachets have been backed stitched; in one example a frayed edge has been introduced. For

66

further finishing touches add bows or fabric flowers, as appropriate.

Lavender balls

Make several of these fragrant lavender balls as gifts for your friends or as bazaar items. Each one can be made quite unique by varying the fabrics and embroidery stitches.

You will need:
Thin cardboard for the 12 templates
Scraps of four kinds of fabric
10cm (4in) of ribbon or cord
Lavender.

To make the patches
Cut out 12 cardboard templates from the trace pattern given. Be careful to trace and cut out the shapes accurately or the patches will not match together. Cut out 12 pieces of material, three shapes from each of the four fabrics, making each piece a little larger than the templates. The fabric should be quite sturdy and of close weave – cottons are ideal – and all four should be of similar weight. Pin a template onto the centre of each piece of fabric on the wrong side (fig. 1). Fold the edges of the material over the template and tack [baste] down (fig. 2), neatening the corners. Remove pins.

To make the ball
Join the patches by placing two together, right sides facing, and oversewing [overcasting] one edge with tiny stitches (fig. 3). Using fig. 4 as an assembly guide, join four shapes around the central patch for one side and repeat with the other six shapes for the second side. Join the two sides together, leaving two seams unstitched. Remove the tacking [basting] and templates, trim any excess fabric, and turn to the right side. Fill ball with lavender and oversew [overcast] the last two seams, inserting the looped cord or ribbon in one corner before closing it up. Choose embroidery threads to tone with the fabrics and, working with two strands, decorate the sides of the ball with straight stitch flowers. French knots, double cross stitch or any other suitable design for your fabric.

Lavender has traditionally been associated with ladies' wardrobes as a way of scenting lingerie and also repelling moths. Make pretty gifts of sachets (opposite) and a ball (left). You don't have to be an expert at sewing, and you can use up leftover scraps of pretty fabric.

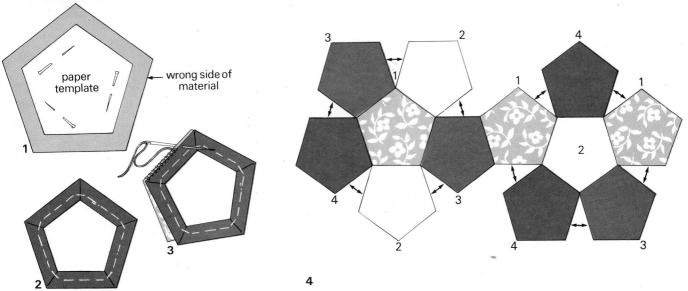

Fantasy flowers

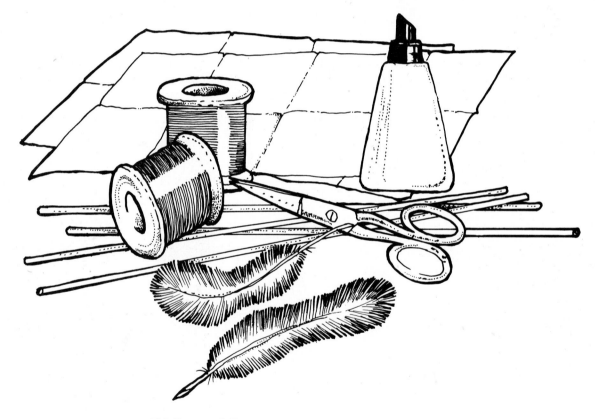

"Mary, Mary, quite contrary,
How does your garden grow?
With silver bells and cockle shells
And pretty maids all in a row."

Tommy Thumb's Pretty Song Book c. 1744

Feather flowers

Flowers from feathers

On close inspection feathers bear a considerable resemblance to the leaves and petals of flowers. The curves of body feathers, for instance, are very like the curve of the petals in many flowers, while the points, oval shape of many wing and tail feathers are amazingly leaf-like. What is different is colour and texture and by using the glossy, often speckled colours characteristic of feathers to mimic blossoms and leaves, many beautiful and exotic looking 'flowers' can be created which, unlike their master images, will last indefinitely.

General rules
To construct a flower, first consider the basic structure that you wish to re-create – that is a seed on a stem with one or more petals around it and, sometimes, with leaves as well.
The seed centres of feather flowers can be made from several things – dried cones, grasses, small dried flowers, beads or bunches of small feathers, such as barbs from ostrich or peacock feathers, or whole small feathers.

Stems
All feather flowers, however made, are mounted on wire stems. Stem wires are obtainable from florists and floral suppliers and are properly called stubb wires. Thin binding wire is normally required as well to secure several components together and to attach them to the false stem (or stubb wire) as shown in fig. 1a. Stems are then covered with special floral tape called gutta percha. Gutta percha sticks to itself and comes in several shades and, like floral wire, it is available from florists and floral suppliers. It is also possible to use strips of crepe paper for covering stems instead of gutta percha.
To cover stems always begin as high up under the 'petals' as possible (fig. 1b). Rotate the stem with your thumb and forefinger until there is enough tape around the base to cover all underpinnings. Then twist the tape in an overlapping spiral down the wire stem and cut it off at the bottom. If crepe paper is used then a dab of glue at the ends will be necessary.

Design
Shape, colour and textures are the three variables, apart from size, which you must consider when creating feather flowers and arranging them.
Since many flowers are quite naturally round in shape there is always the danger, as with real flowers, of making an arrangement which is too repetitive. One way to overcome this limitation is to assemble a few flowers together in a spray or to create a leafy branch to produce a more linear structure.
Do not expect all your flowers to face forwards, they can also bend down or simply turn sideways, in which case their profiles are important and prominent 'stamens' can produce a delicate feature in the arrangement.

Feathers mounted on stems (fig. 1a) then covered with tape (fig. 1b) can make gorgeous fantasy blossoms. The magnificent arrangement (right) is composed entirely of flowers made from different kinds of feathers.

1a
1b

Choosing colour and texture

Choice of colour is personal but colours should blend with the environment in which your arrangement will be placed. Remember also that feathers can be successfully dyed for extra effect.

The textures of feathers play an important part in the design of flowers. Contrast is obtained by using fluffy with smooth or straight with curly. Each quality should appear in moderation, however, particularly the fluff, which in profusion can completely smother a flower design.

Types of arrangements

Unless you particularly choose to make a bowl of matching flowers there are many different kinds you can assemble in one vase.

Feather flowers can also be mixed with dried flowers to make arrangements which vary the colours and textures to an even greater degree.

A selection of feather flowers is given here and each technique can be varied by choice of feathers and seed centres to make other 'species'. By looking at real flowers you can find inspiration for feather ones.

Sunflower

This velvety flower is built on a hemisphere of special floral foam into which the feathers, bead centre and stem wire are pressed.

You will need:

Floral foam ball about 6cm (2½in) in diameter.
1 medium-sized coloured bead for centre.
About 36 striped partridge body feathers.
40 chicken hackle feathers.
3 stubb wires.
Binding wire.
Gutta percha.
All-purpose glue.
Knife.

When selecting feathers, choose only the stripy partridge feathers. If there is any variation in size use the larger ones first. Choose the chicken hackles for similarity of their tips as that is the part that is visible, and cut the base if they are too long.

Floral foam comes in two densities and with the less fine type you will have to use glue to get the feathers to stay put.

Right: A wide range of flowers can be made from feathers. Left to right are a sunflower, leaves, lily, pheasant spray and fircone feather flower.

Making the flower

This flower is worked flat, with no stem until later. Cut the foam ball (fig. 2) in two and place one hemisphere on your working surface.

Start with chicken hackles first and push them into the foam all around the edge to form a circle (fig. 3). If you are using the more porous type of foam you will have to secure the feathers by poking a hole for each one with the end of a stubb wire and giving the feather a dab of glue before pushing it into the foam. This method should secure it.

Note that the flower is worked backwards, that is, starting with the outer

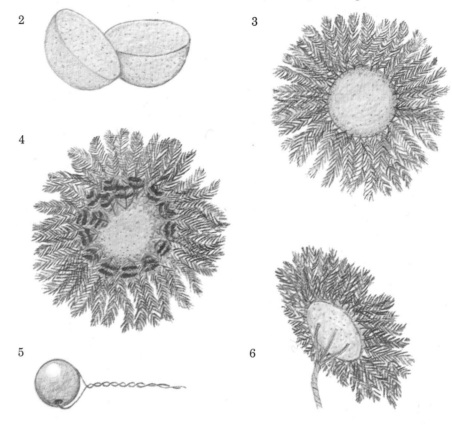

petals and working inwards to the centre ring of petals.

Then make overlapping circles with the partridge feathers (fig. 4) until the entire dome is filled.

Thread the bead with binding wire and twist the ends together (fig. 5) and push the bead into the centre.

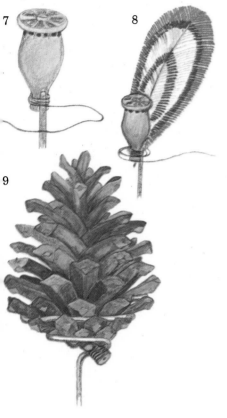

7   8

9

Bind three stubb wires together with gutta percha but leave the top 5cm (2in) separate.

Put some glue on the tip of each wire and push them into the back of the flower (fig. 6).

If necessary you can always cover the back by sticking a few little feathers in to mask the foam.

Leaves

Many varieties of wing and tail feathers can be used to make leaves. The main criterion is that they should be flat. The leaves shown are made from turkey wing feathers.

Leaves normally require cutting, stripping and, to a lesser extent, curling.

Hold the feather in the centre, as close as possible to the cutting place, and cut the top of the feather into a pointed shape with a pair of scissors.

Strip off the lower part of the barbs until only enough remains to make a leaf. The stripped shaft becomes the natural stem.

To make a spray of leaves, attach gutta percha, then bind leaves along another stub wire with gutta percha.

If you want to make an undulating shape to leaves, curve the lower half of the feathers one way and then the tip another.

Lily

This is a good flower to make if you want a large, exotic, tropical type of lily with a dramatic appearance.

Choose some special little firm feathers to make a bunch for the centre; seagull, pigeon wing feathers or those little red feathers from the side of pheasant tails. Then choose some chicken hackles to contrast with the centre feathers, or dye them accordingly to harmonize.

The red curly feathers which form the petals are the soft flat ones from the underside of goose wings, and you will need about 18 of these.

Illustrations showing how to wire different kinds of materials.
Figs. 2-6 show the foam base for a sunflower, and feathers pushed into it until the surface is covered. A wired bead is used as a centre, and the stem wires are twisted together and inserted into the back of flower.
7, 8. Mounting poppy seed and feathers
9. Wiring a fircone.

Strip the fluff from the little centre feathers and most of the barbs from the side of each one. Then curl each feather over to one side to form a slight hook shape. Bind them together tightly at the top of a stubb wire. If you pull the binding wire very tightly the feathers will then kink and fan out.

The hackles are used as they are, but the flat ones require curling. Attach the hackles with continuous binding and arrange them so that they all fan outwards.

Divide the goose feathers into three groups with six feathers in each, then curl the first group just at the top, the second ones half the way down and the last group completely curled.

Use the group of goose feathers curled only at the top first and add each one separately around the centre. Bind very tightly with care and arrange them so that they radiate evenly.

Then add the half-curled feathers in the spaces between the first petals.

Finally add the completely curled feathers, binding with the same wire throughout.

This is a heavy flower which will almost certainly require more than one wire stem to support it; so twist a few together then bind the base of the petals and stem as one. Cover with gutta percha and bend the flower head over so that the explosive centre is clearly visible.

Pheasant flower spray

You will need:
Tiny poppy seedcase.
7 pheasant feathers.
Stubb wire.
Binding wire.
Gutta percha.

Bind a stubb wire to the poppy seed so that the head stands just above the top of the wire (fig. 7) but do not cut off the binding wire from the reel.

Bind each petal separately (fig. 8) to the base of the seed head by successive encirclements with the binding wire. The top of each feather should curve outwards.

The success of your flower depends on binding the petals evenly and tightly and not allowing them to twist around in the process.

Cover the base of the petals and stem with gutta percha.

Make three or four flowers this way then take a stub wire, bind one flower to it with gutta percha, then add the next flower a little further down and then another further on to make a spray. Bind with tape to the end.

Fircone flower

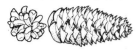

This imaginative combination of natural materials would blend into a dried arrangement or a predominantly feathered one.

You will need:
1 fircome.
7 turkey body feathers.
Stubb wire.
Binding wire.
All-purpose glue.
Gutta percha.

Select your feathers for size and similarity of shape. Some turkey feathers have wide fan-shaped tips and these are the ones to use, so keep the little ones for another flower. The curve also varies enormously and as this must be uniform, do not use the flat specimens. Trim the base of each feather if there is any variation of length, but do not remove any of the fluff.

To put the fircone on a stem make a hook in the tip of a stubb wire and push it into the fircone between the scales at a point where they start to open. Weave the wire between the scales for some way and then make a spiral to support the fircone (fig. 9).

Straighten the wire so that it holds the cone upright.

Push some glue between the scales at the same level as you put the stubb wire in the first place.

Be liberal but not excessive with the amount of glue. The feather must be fixed by the central shaft and not just the fluff.

Now push a row of feathers well into the glue, between the scales so that they encircle the cone. They should all touch each other to form a cup-shaped flower. You may have to hold them in position for a moment until the glue sets hard enough to support.

Finally cover the wire stem with gutta percha.

Below and bottom: Two more kinds of feather flower arrangements. They look particularly good with tall dried grasses added to give height, and also a contrast in texture.

Fabric flowers

Fabric flowers can change a simple outfit into something special – and when you make them yourself they add a further touch of originality at surprisingly little cost.

Wear them on a hat, in the buttonhole of a jacket, on a velvet choker or at the neck of a dress. Quick and easy to make, these decorative accessories will add a flourish to old and new garments alike.

There is an enormous variety of flowers that can be made – from large extravagant cabbage roses to sprays of tiny discreet flowers. You can even make giant specimens of these everlasting fabric flowers and brighten up a room with a flamboyant display of them.

Fabrics

Almost any fabric can be used providing the desired petal shape will hold with starching.

It is advisable to select fabrics that lend themselves to the texture of the flowers. The shiny finish of silk and organza, for example, is particularly suited to roses. Crisp, brightly coloured cottons, on the other hand, are suitable for carnations. The use of gingham gives a gay and variegated effect.

Making sprays

The sprays of small blossoms can be made from almost any fabric. An unusual idea is to use millium, an insulating lining fabric which has a gold and silver finish on either side; as both sides are visible, this has a striking shimmering effect.

Some flowers – a blossom spray, for example – may benefit from the addition of a leaf for a more professional finish. Again, almost any fabric can be used, but the soft texture of velvet is particularly appropriate.

A touch of realism may be added by shading petals and leaves with fabric paint (there are different brands).

These suggestions are guidelines rather than hard and fast rules and are in-tended to inspire, rather than limit you. Adapt the patterns given here, or design your own, to make different flowers. Use real flowers as guides, and be adventurous with fabric textures and colours. If you are a home dressmaker, you can experiment with scraps and even make flowers to match your clothes.

Basic principles

The main technique involved in making fabric flowers is that of 'moulding' the cut-out shapes from flat and lifeless pieces of fabric into realistic petals. The professional artificial flower-maker uses a flower iron to do this – a specially shaped ball on the end of a stick – and a cushion filled with saw-dust on which to work.

Improvised moulds

Beginners who are reluctant to make

These extravagantly coloured fabric flowers make a bright display.

this initial investment may, however, find substitutes in the shape of teaspoons or, better still, melon ball scoops, both of which will provide sufficient curve. Do not use your best spoons as they need to be heated. Use a small firm cushion or ironing pad on which to press the fabric.

To heat the spoon, use a camping gas burner, gas stove, or small blowtorch. It is advisable to use an oven glove when heating the spoon in order to protect your hand. Hold the spoon in the flame for a short while, and test the heat by pressing the spoon on to a scrap of the fabric to be used. The length of time required to heat the spoon will depend on the fabric, just as one needs to regulate an iron according to the material you are pressing.

Place the cut-out petal shape on the cushion and press the back of the spoon onto the fabric to produce the required curve. This may result in a crinkled edge but this can be eliminated later.

Patterns

Patterns are given for two kinds of rose, a blossom for a spray, a carnation and a leaf. It is advisable to make templates in thin cardboard from these trace patterns. You can then draw around the template in pencil on the fabric. Templates ensure accuracy in

cutting out, and, once made, they can be used repeatedly.

You will need:
Relevant card template and pencil.
Sharp scissors.
Small, firm cushion or ironing pad.
Old teaspoon or melon ball scoop.
Latex adhesive.
Florist's stem wire.
Florist's green binding tape for the stems (gutta percha).
Spray starch.
A rose
You will also need:
30cm (12in) by 20cm (8in) of fabric.
Sharp kitchen knife or metal knitting needle.

Trace off these patterns.

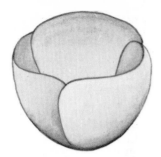

1. Overlap first set of petals.

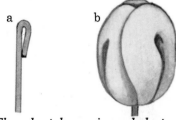

a   b

2. Thread petals on wire and pleat.

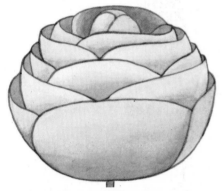

3. Place petals in overlapping layers.

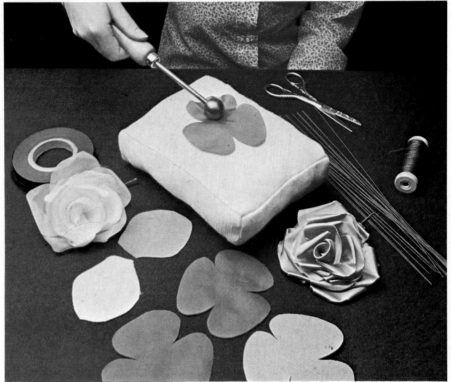

Using the rose pattern with three petals, trace and cut out six shapes in fabric.

Make a small hole in the centre of each shape with the point of the scissors.

Place one cut-out shape on the cushion or ironing pad.

Heat the teaspoon or melon ball scoop and press the back of it onto the centre of each of the three petals so that their edges curve upwards.

Apply a little adhesive to the top left-hand side of each petal and stick them together so that the side edges overlap (fig. 1).

Make a loop in the top of a stem wire (fig. 2a). This is to prevent the first set of petals from slipping off when threaded on.

Thread the first set of petals onto the wire.

Make a pleat in the centre of each petal and secure with adhesive so that the petals close up further into a bud shape (fig. 2b).

Repeat the moulding process with the other five sets of petals.

Apply a little adhesive to the inside centre, around the hole, of each of the five sets of petals.

Thread them one by one onto the stem wire, pushing each one firmly under

Top: A delicate blossom spray and a carnation are fun to make.

Above: Moulding artificial petals with heated melon scoop. A cushion or pad is used to support the fabric.

the previous one. Arrange them so that the petals lie in alternate layers (fig. 3). Leave the adhesive to dry.

Coat the whole flower with spray starch and place to dry on a colour-fast surface, so that the wet flower does not absorb the colour of the surface. Surplus starch will disappear on drying.

Shaping the petals

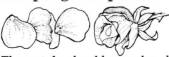

The petals should now be shaped. If you are using fabric that does not fray, use a sharp knife. Holding the blade of the knife between forefinger and thumb,

ease the edges of the open petals one by one over the blade with the thumb so that they curve outwards. If you are using fabric that frays, use a heated metal knitting needle. This will also flatten any crinkled edges.

Cover the stem wire with florist's green binding tape, winding it several times around the wire just below the petals to prevent them from slipping down the stem.

A single petal rose

An equally successful method of making roses, which does not involve the moulding technique, is that of attaching individual petals with florist's binding wire. This method can also be used for many other fabric flowers.

Spray the fabric to be used with spray starch and leave to dry.

Cut one piece of fabric 7.5cm (3in)

square.
Cut out 14 petals from fabric, using the trace pattern given on page 76 for a single petal.
Fold the square of fabric in half diagonally.
Bind the binding wire around the stem wire and then bind in the folded square of fabric, by coiling it into a bud shape and gathering all the raw edges into the binding wire.
Curl the top edges of each petal using a knife or metal knitting needle.
Make a pleat in the base of each petal to form a cup shape.
Join on each petal in turn by binding it on at the base with binding wire. Each petal should overlap half of the previous one.
Cover the base of the final petals where they join the stem with green binding tape and bind the stem.

A tiny blossom

You will need:
12cm (5in) by 6cm (2½in) of suitable fabric.
Pearl stamens.
Florist's binding wire.

Using the blossom pattern, trace and cut out two shapes in fabric.
Make a hole in the centre of each set of petals with the point of the scissors.
Fold four pairs of pearl stamens in half together so that eight pearls are grouped in a bunch (fig. 4a).
Bind them tightly at the point at which they fold to the top of the stem wire with binding wire (fig. 4b).

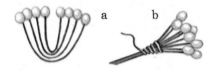

4. Bind pearl stamens to stem wire.

Mould the petals as for the rose. If you are using millium, treat the gold side as the upper side for one set of petals, and the silver side for the other set. In this way, both the gold and silver finishes will be visible in one blossom.
Thread the first set of petals onto the stem wire and push it up firmly under the stamens.
Apply a dab of adhesive around the central hole of the second set of petals, and thread it onto the stem wire, pushing it up firmly under the first set.
Bind the stem with florist's binding tape, ensuring that there is enough tape just below the flower head to hold it in place.

Spray the finished flower with spray starch and leave to dry.
You can make up a blossom spray with any number of these tiny flowers, depending on how large a spray you require. Arrange the flowers into a group, add a leaf if desired, and bind the stems together with binding tape.

A carnation

You will need:
30cm (12in) by 20cm (8in) of fabric.
Pinking shears.
One small artificial fruit.
Florist's binding wire.

Using the carnation pattern given, cut out six shapes.
Trim the edges of three of the circles with pinking shears.
Trim away 1.5cm (½in) from the edges of the other three circles so that they are smaller than the first three.
Make a hole in the centre of each circle of fabric with the point of the scissors.
Join the stem of the artificial fruit to the top of a stem wire by binding the two together with florist's binding wire (fig. 5).

5. Bind artificial fruit to stem wire.

Cut three slits in each circular shape at equal intervals as shown in fig.6a.
Working on each circle in turn, apply a little adhesive to both inner edges of each slit and stick them together so that the flat circles of fabric become cup-shaped (fig. 6b).

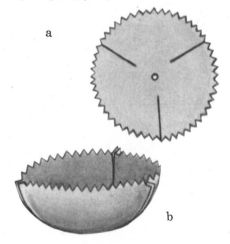

6. Make each circle cup-shaped.

Apply a little adhesive around the central hole of each set of petals.
Thread the three smaller sets onto the stem wire first, pushing them up firmly under the artificial fruit. Thread on the other three sets of petals.
Bind the stem with florist's binding tape, wrapping it around the top of the stem, just below the flower, several times to prevent the petals from slipping down the stem.
Spray the completed flower with spray starch and leave to dry.

A leaf

You will need
15cm (6in) of velvet ribbon 3cm (1¼in) wide.
7.5cm (3in) of iron-on hem tape with adhesive on both sides, 3cm (1¼in) wide.
Florist's stem wire.
Ironing board and iron.
Florist's binding tape.

Place the velvet ribbon on the ironing board, right side down. Place the hem tape on half the length of the ribbon.
Position the stem wire diagonally across the hem tape, with one end meeting the corner of the tape at the centre of the length of ribbon.
Fold the other half of the ribbon over the hem tape and wire, and press all the layers together with a warm iron so that the wire and hem tape are sandwiched between the two layers of velvet (fig. 7).

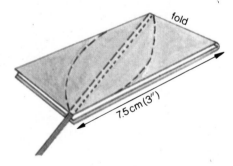

7. Wire is sandwiched between velvet.

Using the leaf pattern, draw shape on the velvet, making the tip of the leaf correspond with the tip of the wire (see fig. 7).
Cut out the leaf shape.
Bind the stem wire with florist's binding tape.
The stem wire sandwiched between the two layers of velvet is equivalent to the central vein of a leaf. It gives body to the artificial leaf and enables you to bend it in any direction you wish, or give it extra shape.

Clay flowers

You can make beautiful flowers from clay, which is obtainable from craft stores.

To make the posy

You will need:
½kg (1lb) clay
Paints, varnish and brushes for decorating
Green-coated wire for stems
Pliers for cutting and bending wire
Small vase and plasticine to complete display.

Begin by shaping the flowers from lumps of clay about the size of a large marble. Petals can be flattened out between the fingers, moistened and attached to the knob-shaped flower centre. Bell shapes look particularly effective with the edges turned over and outwards.
As an alternative to shaping the flower with the fingers, press the clay out flat, then slice it with a small, sharp knife to give a serrated leaf effect. Petals can be sliced to shape and curled inwards or outwards, or trimmed with the point of a scalpel to give a delicate, frilled edge.
When the flower is completed, use the point of a pencil to bore a hole through the centre, to take the wire stem which is inserted later. Leave the flowers to dry out thoroughly before painting them.

Painting the flowers
Painted decoration can be either naturalistic or the exact opposite – choose subtle, delicate flower tones or bright, primary colours. When the paint is completely dry, paint the flowers with clear varnish to prevent them chipping.

Arranging the flowers
Select a suitable small vase for the arrangement and place a knob of plasticine in the bottom. Hook over one end of a suitable length of wire and pass the other end down through the centre of the flower. Pull the wire through so that the hooked end is taut against the flower centre, then make a kink in the wire, hard against the neck of the flower to hold it in place.

Daisy ear-rings
Instead of grouping the flowers together to form a posy, try making a pair of daisies as ear-rings – jeweller's findings are easily fixed to the back with fast drying adhesive. Brooches are excellent projects – a large stylized flower can be pinned to a hat brim, a cluster of small flowers can be worn on a lapel or waistband. A realistic red rose, for example, is an unusual brooch, and is very simple to make even for the most inexperienced person.

To make the rose brooch

You will need:
Lump of clay about the size of a ping-pong ball
Paints and brush
2.5cm (1in) brooch finding.

Use your fingers to press out a strip of clay about 15cm (6in) long and 2cm (¾in) wide. The edges should be slightly uneven, as this adds to the natural effect.
Begin rolling up the strip tightly at first to represent the centre of the flower, then more loosely to represent the outer petals. Continue rolling until the flower is complete, then pinch off the remainder of the strip.
Moisten the inner edge of the strip and press it firmly against the flower to secure it. Turn the rose over and, with a moistened fingertip, flatten the back to make a smooth surface.
Leave the rose to dry, then paint it. When paint is dry, use fast drying adhesive to secure the finding in place on the back.

Happy flowers—made in clay.

Flowers from the seashore

Victorian ladies of leisure used to spend hours patiently making shell flowers from a great number of tiny shells. These arrangements, many of which still survive under glass domes, can be copied, but it is possible to produce attractive results more simply. Shells which are translucent lend themselves particularly well to use in three-dimensional objects such as flowers or lampshades, because light can pass through them easily.

The different shapes of shells can be used for different parts of a flower arrangement. Flat shells make ideal petals which can be wired or glued to one another at their hinges. They can also be used to form a base for a flower – a container to hold a small amount of cement filler such as Poly-filla [spackling putty] in which 'petals' are embedded. Coiled shells and cowries can be used for buds when mounted individually on wire stems. Pointed shells and razor shells can be wired and used as bulrushes. Different types of coral can be used to represent foliage. When you have selected a number of shells for use in a particular arrangement, you may wish to colour them. Lacquer paints of the type used for modelling are suitable, either to colour the whole shell or part of it. Another way of colouring shells is to dip them into a pan of boiling fabric dye and water until the colour has been absorbed.

Three flowers

The three flowers in the photograph resemble a dahlia, a poppy and a bul-rush. You could make several of each of these and arrange them all together in a vase, or separately.

You will need:
One double razor shell.
Seven banded tops or similarly shaped univalves.
One large limpet.
One small limpet.
Seven small scallops.
A cement filler [Spackling putty] mixed with water to a pliable paste.
Six floral stem (stub) wires.
Thin floral binding wire, at least 1.5m

(5ft) long.
Gutta percha, scissors, a pointed instrument such as a compass.
Lacquer paint [modelling paint] such as Humbrol's, and brushes (optional).

The bulrush
To make the 'bulrush', cover a stem wire with gutta percha (this is floral tape which sticks to itself) and then bend the top of the wire to form a hook about 5cm (2in) long.
Open the two valves of the razor shell carefully and put a teaspoonful of the mixed paste inside one end of one valve. Embed the hooked end of the wire in the paste [spackling] and close the

shell. If necessary, twist a piece of binding wire around the shell to hold the two valves together until the paste [spackling] has dried.

The dahlia
To make the dahlia, cover a stem wire with gutta percha. Take the large limpet and coat its outside with a liberal amount of paste [spackling]. Bend one end of the wire around to make a loop which is slightly smaller than the diameter of the limpet. Embed the loop in the paste [spackling] on the limpet (fig. 1).

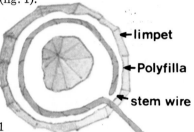

1

Below: Dahlia, poppy and bulrush are all made from shells.

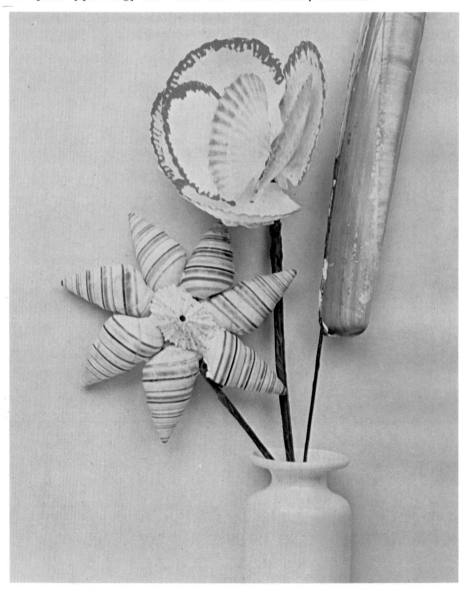

Arrange seven banded tops around the limpet, pressing them into the paste [spackling] so that they are evenly spaced and with their pointed ends facing outwards.

Place a small limpet over the centre of the flower, on top of the large limpet. Leave to dry.

Take one more stem wire and bind it to the first looped wire with gutta percha. You will find that the weight of the flower head requires this extra support.

The poppy

To make the 'poppy', take the seven scallop shells and, if you wish, paint the edge of each shell. The flower has seven shell petals.

Using a pointed instrument such as the sharp end of a pair of compasses [compass], make two holes one above the other in the base of the shell.

Cut 14 lengths of binding wire, each about 10cm (4in) long, two for each shell. Thread one length of wire through the top hole of one of the shells and another length through both holes. Pull the ends through until they are level and twist them together (fig. 2).

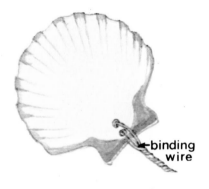

Repeat the process with the other scallops so that they all have short twisted wire stems.

Twist the thin wires on one shell around one end of a stem wire (fig. 3). Add the other six shells to the stem wire in the same way, arranging the seven shells so that they are evenly spaced with three shells in the centre and four outside. Place two more stem wires beside the first stem wire and bind them all together with gutta percha.

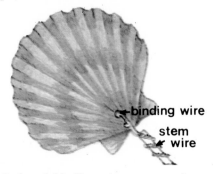

3. Attach binding wires to stem wire.

Cockle shell design

This incorporates two cockle shells which are used as a base.

You will need:

15 small wedge shells, and tiny abalone chips, seven keyhole limpets (which have a hole in the centre), five pieces of scallops, 19 cowries and two cockles. Seven olive shells.

Three compressed cotton wool balls, which are known as 'puffballs'.

Green and red lacquer paint, brushes.

Glue, Polyfilla paste [Spackling putty], Florists' foam.

Stem wires and binding wire about 3m (9ft) long, gutta percha. Hacksaw.

To make a five-petalled flower, cover a stem wire with gutta percha and glue it to a puffball. Coat the ball with glue. Press the backs of the wedge shells round it to form petals; press abalone chips in the centre to cover the puffball. Make three of these flowers.

To make the limpet flowers, cut a 15cm (6in) length of binding wire and fold it in half. Put some paste [spackling] into the cleft of an olive shell and press the fold of the wire into the shell. When the paste [spackling] is dry, thread the ends of the wire through the limpet from the inside and make a twist at the back of the limpet to secure it in position (fig. 4), before straightening the rest to use as a stem. Make seven of these flowers.

To make the 'leaves', use a hack saw to trim the scallop pieces to leaf shapes. Cover five stem wires with gutta percha and glue one to the back of each leaf shape. Paint each leaf green with lacquer paint.

To make the cowrie sprays, use 11

The completed design is very pretty.

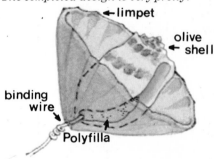

4. Thread the wire through the limpet.

5. Wrap wire around each cowrie.

cowries. Cut 11 15cm (6in) lengths of binding wire and wrap one around each shell (fig. 5), twisting the ends together to form the stems. Dip each one into the paint and leave to dry. Assemble into three sprays of three shells and one of two by simply twisting the ends of the binding wire together.

To make the container which holds the flowers, take the larger cockle and put a large blob of paste [spackling] on its apex. Place the remaining cowries in a circle around the edge of the blob and set the other cockle in their centre, concave side up on top of the first cockle. Fix a piece of florists' foam to the centre of the second cockle and push the stems of the flowers into it, to form a pleasing arrangement.

Making paper flowers

Crepe paper has always been popular for making flowers because it can be stretched and formed to suit whatever flower shape you like to make.

It has quite different qualities from tissue paper and the more time you spend coaxing and shaping it the more interesting it becomes. Even the cheapest brand of crepe paper will expand over half as much again, which gives plenty of scope for modelling flowers – from roses to arum lilies. It is also easily wrapped around wire to make a perfect covering for stems.

Crepe paper is bought in lengths of about 3m (10ft) and this is called a fold. The kind generally available is single crepe which is 50cm (20in) wide. Crepe paper is also manufactured especially for flower-making in two layers bonded together, 25cm (10in) wide, and this is known as double crepe. Unfortunately, it is now sold through very few outlets.

Preparing flower parts

Crepe paper stretches one way only – lengthways. The grain, that is the small lines, run along the width. The petals and leaves in most flowers have the stretch going across and the grain running downwards. Hold a fold of paper firmly in one hand and, with the other hand, cut strips off with sharp scissors – parallel to the edge of the fold (fig. 1) and cutting across the grain of the paper.

For stem bindings cut strips 13mm ($\frac{1}{2}$in) to 2.5cm (1in) in width.

For petals cut 10cm (4in) widths for small flowers and 15cm (6in) widths for medium sized flowers.

Always cut crepe paper strips across the grain to ensure that the stretch goes in the right direction.

1

Covering wire with crepe paper strips

When practising this technique the wire will not be attached to a flower but, when you are actually flower-making, it could be.

First put a little glue at the top of the wire or, if it is attached to a flower, around the base of the flower and calyx (fig. 2). Wrap the binding around the top of the wire very tightly two or three times.

Holding the paper between the thumb and forefinger of either the left or right hand – whichever you find the easiest – twirl the wire around with the other hand.

2a

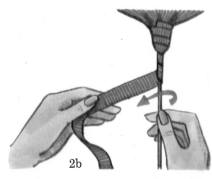

2b

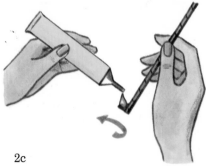

2c

Guide the binding diagonally down, stretching the paper to make it tight. When you reach the bottom, break off the paper, glue and stick down.

Cutting fringes

Cut a crepe paper strip as described, making it the width you want the fringe to be plus 2.5cm (1in) as a base for attaching to the stem wire (fig. 3). Unfold the strip and fold it in half, fold

3a

3b

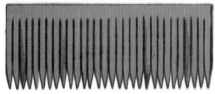

3c

it again, then fold it once more. Pin it once or twice to keep it in place. Start cutting the fringe along the grain, making the cuts about 13mm ($\frac{1}{2}$in) apart or closer if you want. You can leave the ends of the fringe square or cut them into points.

There is an alternative way of cutting a fringe. If your hands are fairly strong and your scissors are sharp, you can cut a fringe straight into the crepe paper strip without unfolding it. This is obviously the quickest method and one worth trying when you have more confidence and experience.

Assembling the flower

Bending the wire top. The top of the stem wire is often bent to prevent the flower centre and petals falling off. Take the top of the wire between thumb and forefinger, turn it over 6mm ($\frac{1}{4}$in) and bend it back as close to the wire as possible. This is easier to do with a pair of pliers (fig. 4).

4

Wiring petals onto stem wire

This is done with florists' wire and takes a little practice. You may find it helps to put a little glue at the base of the paper before you start. Hold the paper (whether it is the centre of a flower, or petals) against the stem wire, wind the florists' wire around a few times and hook the end of the stem wire over the wound wire to secure it (fig. 5). Pull very tight and continue winding around and down the stem a little way before breaking off.

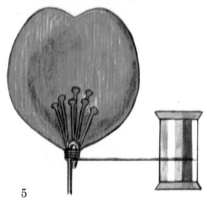

5

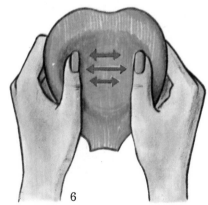

6

Shaping petals

Place your thumbs and fingers on either side of petal. Stretch the paper widthways gently with your thumbs, producing a cupped shape (fig. 6).
Shaping petals with scissors is easy to do. Hold the petal with one hand and the

Learn how to cut and shape crepe paper (figs. 1-8) to make beautiful flowers like the poppies and sunflowers (above).

opened scissor blades in the other. With the inside of the scissors blade behind the paper, gently scrape across the underside of the paper, as shown (fig. 7), to give a gentle curve.
Curling petals around a pencil is another method. For a tighter curve, wrap the petal edge around a pencil or orange stick very tightly, then withdraw it (fig. 8).

Artichoke flowers
These are one of the simplest crepe paper flowers to make and you can use the same techniques to make many different types of flowers. The centre is composed of several strips of fringes that have been wrapped around the stem wire. The fringe ends have been pinched and ruffled up to soften their

7

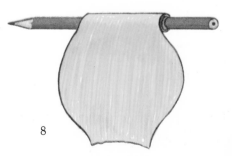

8

outlines. These flowers make amusing and attractive decorations and mix well with dried grasses.

You will need:
Four folds of crepe paper – suggested colours are one mauve, one yellow and one white for the centre and one brown or green for the outer circles of petals. This is enough for two flowers.
50cm (20in) of 1.6mm (14 gauge) stem wire and green crepe paper
Florists' wire
Large tube of PVA glue
Tape measure

To make centres cut a strip about 16cm (6½in) wide, as described in preparing flower parts, from each of mauve, white and yellow folds of paper.
Unwrap each, cut fringe and cut each into three equal pieces. These are now ready to wrap around the centre of the flower. (Some strips will be left over for use on the next flower.)
Take a yellow fringe piece and fold into four. Put a dab of glue on the base and place the stem wire on the glue (fig. 9).
Making sure that the base of the crepe thicknesses are flat and level, roll the paper around the wire (fig. 10).
Secure in place with florists' wire (figs. 11 and 12).
Continue to add fringed strips – first white, then mauve, then yellow. You can stop at three strips or use a fourth strip if you want the flower centre to be larger.

To make the outer petal

Cut a 23cm (9in) wide strip from the brown or green paper. From this strip cut off four 61cm (24in) lengths. Refold three of the four lengths. Take the first folded length and trim 2.5cm (1in) off width to make a 20.5cm (8in) wide strip. Trim another one to 17.5cm (7in) and the fourth to 15cm (6in). These form the four circles of outer petals.
Fold each strip neatly in concertina folds about 3cm (1¼in) wide and, when you have done about ten folds, stop and trim off the excess with scissors. Cut a pointed shape as shown (fig. 13).
Unfold the strips, then bunch base into tiny pleats as shown (fig. 14). Also shape the petals by cupping.
Working with the 23cm (9in) wide strip, put dabs of glue all the way along the base and lay the flower centre down on the glue (fig. 14).
Wrap the petal strip firmly in place at the base (fig. 15). Hold it for a few seconds until the glue sets, making sure you keep the flower circular and even with a good shape (fig. 16).

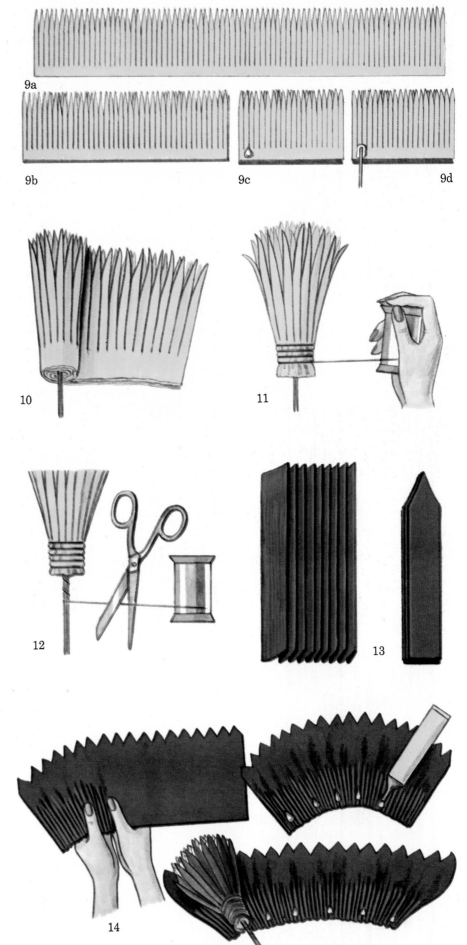

9a

9b   9c   9d

10   11

12   13

14

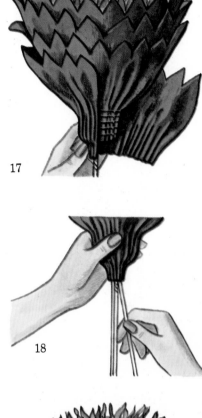

17

18

19

One of the most unusual and dramatic designs for paper flowers are these stunning artichokes. Created from layers of fringed crepe paper (figs. 9-19) they are not very difficult to make, and are so attractive.

Cover the wires with a 5cm (2in) wide crepe paper strip as described in flower making techniques, pulling strip really tight.

The final touches
Ruffle and spread out the centre fringes and twist them together with your fingertips.
Work the crepe paper a little to make it look more natural.
Flatten the points of the petals firmly out and down (fig. 19).
Curve the stem slightly towards the top near the flower.

15

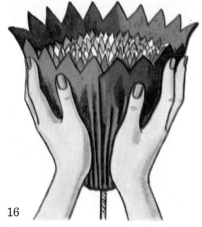

16

Continue in the same way with the 20.5cm (8in) strip, followed by the 17.5cm (7in) strip and then the 15cm (6in) strip, keeping the base even but graduating to shorter petals on the outside of the flower (fig. 17).
Strengthen the stem by adding two more stem wires. Lay the two new wires against the first wire, pushing them up into the flower base (fig. 18).

Realistic paper roses

This chapter shows you how to make lifelike paper roses which are constructed in a similar way to real ones. The petal patterns have been closely copied from nature and each flower is made up of about 26 petals – though a real rose will often have many more! The flowers illustrated have been made from single crepe paper in order to achieve the most realistic effect. You could also try making them in tissue paper, using the same method but omitting the petal shaping procedure. You will find the results just as pretty.

Old-fashioned roses

These roses have been made in white, with green for the calyx, leaves and stems. They have been lightly tinted with a little oil paint to give them extra, subtle colouring. This is quite simple and if you wish to do the same thing, you must add a few more materials to your shopping list.

You will need:
Single crepe paper in white and green – a fold of each makes several roses.
26cm (10in) of 1mm (gauge 18) wire for stem wires.
Florists' wire.
Yellow stamens or sisal string and yellow powder colour.
PVA glue and paper scissors.

Small tube of rose madder oil paint.
White spirit.
Sable brush – medium size is best.

Petals

There are two sizes of petal patterns to make. Smaller roses have about 24 petals cut from the small pattern and the bigger roses have 16 small petals and about eight to ten large outside.

Stamens
If you are using string, unravel and straighten a length from the ball, then cut off about 2.5cm (1in) for each flower. Dip the tips of the string in a mixture of PVA glue and yellow powder colour.
Trace the patterns in figs. 1a and b on to thin paper and stick them down on light cardboard.
When dry, cut out and label them.
Bend over the top of the stem wire for 13mm ($\frac{1}{2}$in). Fold a few stamens in half and bind to the stem tightly with florists' wire (fig. 2).

Prepare the petals
First cut the fold of white crepe paper

Make this romantic paper rose.

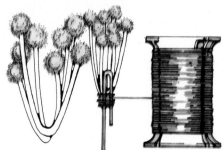

2. Binding stamens to the stem wire.

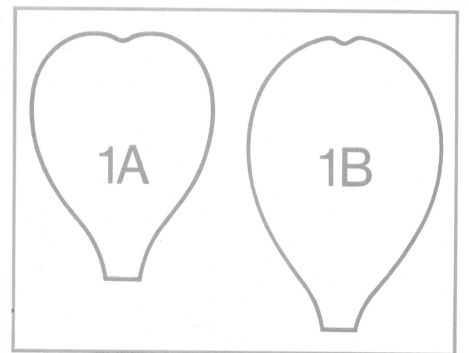

3. Petal patterns pinned to paper.

in half. Unwind one half and fold that in half, then again, then once more.

You now have eight layers which you must hold together by pinning at each corner.

Draw around the petal patterns lightly with a pencil, as close together as possible, then pin each drawing in the centre (fig. 3). Use tiny pins if you have them. Prepare the quantity you will require for all your flowers and cut them out carefully.

Shape the petals

Take a group and remove the pin. Take four petals and shape them all together. Cup the centre, curl the edges over a pencil and gently stretch the curls (fig. 4).

Make enough petals for at least one complete flower.

Fixing petals onto stem

Take four prepared petals and separate them. Cup and shape each one a little more. Lay them down in a line so that they overlap and pleat the lower edge as shown (fig. 5). When overlapping the four petals in a line, dab a blob of glue at the bottom of each one.

Allow the glue to set a little then pick them up together and wrap them around the stamens and stem wire. Secure with florists' wire (fig. 6).

Do the same with four more petals, wrapping them around the inside petals in a continuous spiral. Do at least 16 petals in this way (fig. 7), spreading the petals further apart as you reach the outside of the flower.

Continue adding petals until satisfied with the shape of your flowers.

Calyx, stems and leaves

Trace off the calyx pattern and cut calyx pieces from green paper, cutting one for each rose (fig. 8).

Shape the calyx by stretching across the base of the points and rolling the tips between the fingers. Dab the base with glue and stick around the bottom of the flower (fig. 9).

Cover the stem wire with narrow green strips of paper as described in the chapter on general flower making techniques (page 82). Curve stem wires.

If you like the effect of a few leaves, add some to the stem, cutting them smaller and more pointed than the petals.

Painting

White spirit must be used as the medium when colouring crepe paper, as water causes it to disintegrate.

Pick up a minute quantity of oil paint with the brush and, working on a tile or pottery saucer, dilute with white spirit. Make sure to mix them very thoroughly, then brush a little onto a spare piece of white crepe paper to test the colour. Add more spirit if it is too dark and more paint if it is too pale.

Paint the flowers all over with the wash. Make the centre of the roses a little darker with stronger colour and add this same dark colour to the tips of the calyx, the stems and leaves.

After painting, place the flowers near an open window to help get rid of the strong smell of the spirit, but don't worry about this as it will disappear in a day or two.

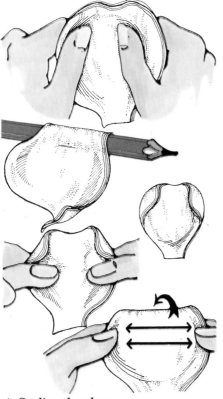

4. Curling the edges of the petals.

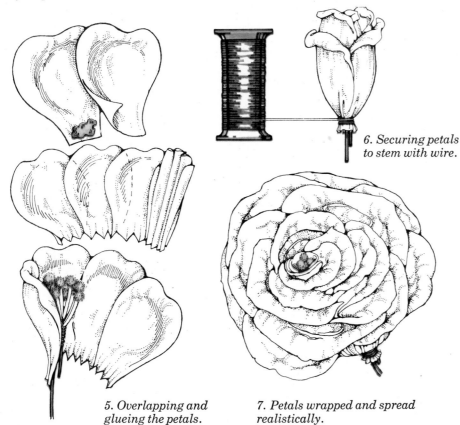

5. Overlapping and glueing the petals.

6. Securing petals to stem with wire.

7. Petals wrapped and spread realistically.

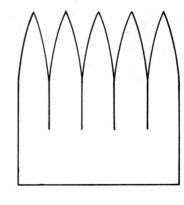

8. Make one calyx for each rose.

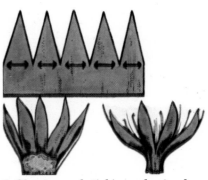

9. Shaping and sticking calyx in place.

Index